TROY KIRBY

THE SPORTSCASTER'S NOTEBOOK

2022 edition

ISBN: 978-1-947863-20-0 (Hardcover edition)
ISBN: 978-1-947863-19-4 (Paperback edition)
ISBN: 978-1-947863-18-7 (Kindle edition)

Library of Congress Control Number: 2022930133

Printed and bounded in the United States of America.
First printing, original version, May 2008
Second printing, new version, January 2022

The following people dedicated themselves toward helping The Sportscaster's Notebook 2022 Edition come to fruition:

Chris Thompson
Jason Behenna
Justin Kesterson
Wade Fisher
Vance Dawson

Author's Note
What A Long Strange Trip It's Been Since 2008.

Fourteen years ago, I published *The Sportscaster's Notebook* on Amazon's *then* new platform, Createspace. It was cobbled together from a bunch of notes that I had created over the past decade prior, mainly out of frustration of not finding much credible play-by-play training content from other texts. Frankly, I was shocked. What shocked me even more was the response. Over the past 14 years, I've received countless e-mails, watched as a little self-published book that had barely any grammar or professional editing, took off. It didn't even have a cover. All of the no-no's that self-publishing is today suggests that *The Sportscaster's Notebook* wouldn't sell, and yet it did.

Now, 14 years later, I've decided to continually commit myself to updating the book when it needs it. That means re-writing the original text, having it professionally edited, adding a cover, and including a few more chapters. Things have changed since 2008 when I first published this book. That thing called social media has taken over, radio broadcasting is a bare-bones operation, and video livestreaming is really hitting its stride. That means that sports play-by-play is more necessary than ever. And I feel that *The Sportscaster's Notebook* should be updated, rebuilt, and reformatted to meet that need.

Back in 2008, I had trained several play-by-play announcers using those notes that became *The Sportscaster's Notebook*. I laid out the entire book in Adobe's InDesign 1. Which didn't reformat well into e-book form, and didn't really work well in book form in some ways. Now, looking back, I want to thank those who stayed with it, purchased *The*

THE SPORTSCASTER'S NOTEBOOK

Sportscaster's Notebook, found solace in its teaching, looking past the grammatical flaws for what a good teaching text it was. That's why I felt I owed it to at least update the book, as a new generation discovers it.

I never thought that I would sell 15 copies, let alone over 1,500+ since the book was published. Sports is the last live shared experience in the world. Notice how sports broadcasting became even more needed after COVID-19, when anything that could be broadcast was broadcast, and definitely required a sportscaster in order to broadcast it. That's why I felt *The Sportscaster's Notebook* deserved a new edition.

Sincerely,

Troy Kirby

Table of Contents

Justin Kesterson

*Point of View
Fmr. Student of
The Sportscaster's Notebook*

As a Seattle University graduate student in 2007, I was able to put a number of the tips and tricks inside *The Sportscaster's Notebook* into action, producing the first-ever women's college basketball livestream for my university. I am still in disbelief that it has been over 15 years since Troy Kirby handled me a stack of notes which later became this book. I recall Bill Hogan, Seattle University athletic director, remarking that he was amazed Kirby had managed to put it together in book form. The fact that this book has sold over 1,500 copies since 2008 shows you that the information is being sought out by those who want to bring play-by-play to their local area or who want to get into the field of sportscasting.

Back in 2007, I was paired with another graduate student, who has now gone on to become a high school athletic director in Colorado. We worked together with Troy Kirby to create a product that expanded the reach of our NCAA Division II athletics program as it started to transition to NCAA Division I membership. Our broadcasts also created an advertising revenue stream for the athletic department that didn't exist before, all at a low cost to the program. Following much of the information inside this book, two amateur broadcasters were able to have fun and seem as though they knew what they were doing.

Prior to any broadcast we would do a couple of hours of show prep as outlined in the book, researching as much as possible about the upcoming opponents to try and know as much about them as we did about our own team. The information helped us tremendously as we became stronger writers, and our broadcasts became better as we were prepared to fill dead air during the broadcasts with unique stories or stats about the players and teams. During the 2007-08 women's basketball season, we traveled on the road to several of the local opponents' gyms along the I-5 and I-90 corridor, providing the parents of Seattle University student-athletes with the ability to listen to a livestream when they were physically unable to travel with the team. We averaged about 100-150 consistent listeners for our livestream, at a time when livestreams weren't really a thing yet. At one point in the season, when the regular men's basketball play-by-play crew was unavailable, my broadcast partner and I did the men's basketball games as well. Putting in the work earlier with the women's basketball broadcasts allowed us to earn the ability to bring our show to the men's basketball games later.

Interviews can be tough, especially when a team is down at the half or after a loss, but the simple questions listed in this book were a great starting point for us. We learned how to ask key questions as well as how to improve our writing skill. The notebook helped me personally grow in these areas, which I later used while working at the Seattle Mariners as part of their public relations team. Everything is about growth and putting what you've learned to good use in various ways moving forward.

I've had the unique privilege to do the play-by-play and color analyst gigs. Following the advice in this book for both positions was vital. As the play-by-play broadcaster, it's important to know the little details which can make your broadcast sound more professional. The diagrams and exercises in this book will help even the most novice broadcaster feel more confident in their first broadcast.

As the color analyst it was important to know the game and to be able to feed off my partner to make the broadcast as seamless as possible. Following the simple steps in here made me better at what I was doing. As the book indicates, all of the information is transferable to a number of sports. I was able to take the same information from the 2007-08 Seattle University basketball season and apply it to the 2008 spring softball season, airing the first webcasts of our softball team as well. Think about the impact made for Seattle University player parents who could not attend as well as general softball fans. It helped me generate enough confidence to know that I could do a play-by-play broadcast when needed, regardless of the area and circumstance. From 2009-11, as the Assistant Director of Operations and Media Relations at Montana State Billings Athletics, I had a firm understanding of how to help media because of my play-by-play experience at Seattle University. *The Sportscaster's Notebook* breaks down the information so that anyone can start their own broadcasting career or help those who are already in it.

Sincerely,

Justin Kesterson
Assistant Executive Director – Activities & Eligibility / Washington Interscholastic Athletics Association - 2018-19 2A South Puget Sound League Athletic Director of the Year

Jason Behenna

Legendary
Sports Information Director

Shortly after I started my tenure as sports information director at Seattle University in 2006, the school announced its transition from NCAA Division II to NCAA Division I.

I knew that some sort of broadcast situation would be established for the men's basketball team, and I started thinking about the possibility of creating something similar for the women's basketball program.

Thanks to the insight of Troy Kirby, who had completed a graduate assistantship within sports information and was now coming up with a ticketing plan to start generating revenue, the idea of a live audio stream for women's basketball was born. Justin Kesterson and Ben Peterson, who joined the Seattle U athletic staff in the fall of 2007 as graduate assistants, showed interest in broadcasting the games, both home and away when possible.

For both Troy and me, a professional-sounding broadcast was the only way to go. We both heard too many unprofessional play-by-play announcers over the years and believed that they detracted from the broadcast. Troy met with Justin and Ben several times leading up to their first broadcast, going over the fundamentals that are detailed throughout this book. We figured out the technical aspects of the livestream broadcasts and established a way for supporters of the Redhawk women's basketball program to follow along if they could not come to campus.

Because we found the right people that took this seriously, Troy and I did not have to worry about offending our listeners. Simple things went a long way towards establishing credibility for our broadcasts, like pronouncing individual names for both teams correctly, using the in-game statistics feeds to add information, and conducting interviews that were informative and fun at the appropriate times. Looking back at my past press releases from this time period, I always made sure to let our fans know when the next broadcast would take place. I was proud of the job Justin, Ben, and later Chris McCullough, another Seattle U graduate assistant, were doing in this role.

Now, 15 years later, I find myself going through a similar process, potentially establishing an audio component to our video livestreams at my current place of employment, Regis College in Massachusetts. Pam Roecker, the Dean of Athletics at Regis College, is in her 20th year as a color analyst for women's collegiate basketball, currently working games within the Northeast Conference, America East Conference, and Big East Conference. She wants to start training students to become broadcasters for Regis Pride athletic events, with basketball as the probable first sport.

The technology is available to quickly and easily include audio to our existing video streams. Once again, I will be looking for professionalism and work ethic. Our student-athletes and coaches, as well as those who support them and will be the ones tuning into these broadcasts, deserve a good product. That does not mean I am looking for broadcasters on the level of Mike Breen or Hubie Brown right at the start, but those who do participate in any broadcast I am overseeing will have a fundamental base to work from.

One thing I will make sure to tell my broadcasters is to relax and have fun. We are not competing with anyone, there is no ratings war, at least where we are at the NCAA Division III level, and our goal is to simply enhance our already-existing video offering with an intelligent and thoughtful description of the action. Similar to how I treat graduate assistants within my office, this will be a tool for advancement, especially for someone who wants to make broadcasting a career. With the explosion of major online outlets such as ESPN+ and FloSports, play-by-play announcing opportunities are more plentiful now than they ever were before. With the right training and mentorship, I believe anyone who puts in the work can become a sports broadcaster.

Sincerely,
Jason Behenna, SID at Regis College

Cheat Sheet

Let's sum up a lot of the sportscasting theory used in this notebook. Way too often, several books on sportscasting merely give a few tips, but also a lot of war stories, which aren't as helpful. They don't cut down to the chase. If you decide to read this cheat sheet and nothing else, it may help a little until you finally decide to digest the book.

However, you will not develop your skills into a craft to become a great sportscaster until you read the book cover to cover, and understand everything inside.

1. A show prep artist continues to develop their craft.

2. Sportscasters have exceptional writing skills.

3. Reading **OUTLOUD** helps build **LIVE** copy reading skills.

4. Understanding history and development of the game is a must to be a great sportscaster.

5. Sportscasters desire to consistent improve their craft.

6. Sportscasting means mistakes that are learned from, not avoided.

7. Learning to practice from game tape builds skills.

8. Over-delivering for your sponsors is must in today's world.

9. Hit your target audience effectively. Do not ignore them.

10. You are not the show, only part of it.

11. Dress professionally to be taken seriously.

12. Sportscasters know to make the broadcast fun and exciting.

13. Do not speculate on injuries without confirmation from the team.

14. Take your broadcast and craft seriously. Always.

Chapter One

*Hobby, Employee
or
Independent Contractor*

The primary concern for any sportscaster is how to break into the industry. Sportscasting is one of the last great industries where you get more gigs by hustling. It is an elite field. You cannot sit around, expecting to have the phone ring, if you are unwilling or unable to produce content and hustle. Too often, that's where the line of demarcation lies. Talent is a wasted opportunity and usually another word for "under-achiever." A lot of people are talented. A lot of talent exists out there, but without continually training, developing and honing your talent into a skill, talent is meaningless and worthless. Getting a job, breaking into the sportscasting world, is showcasing that you are willing to make certain sacrifices, and that you believe in your talent developing into a skill.

Really, after that point, with a few tips along the way, the rest is easy. As long as you continue to hustle. Many talented people waste time, energy and focus without getting into their real calling in life. Specifically because they are unable or unwilling to learn how to break into the field of their choice. Let's dispense with the B.S. nonsense that seems like a page-filler for most textbooks, instead focusing on how to make this one golden opportunity available to anyone who thinks "I can do that" whenever listening to someone else do play-by-play for a sporting event. Chances are, they are right, they can "do that" too. Sometimes better, sometimes worse. It depends on whether they are willing and able to out-hustle everyone else who wants to do play-by-play too.

While this book tends to focus on the sport of basketball, encompassing the arena of the sportscaster, the context of the book allows the reader to use whatever recommendations in an expandable format, enough to cover most sporting events being broadcast today. And it should be pointed out, that all of those sports broadcasts, even esports and drone racing, require play-by-play broadcasters in order to do it. Everything else can be cut down during modernization, but if the sportscaster isn't presenting the details, well, it doesn't really click with the viewer, especially during livestreaming events.

In order to develop these lines of thought, each subject will be presented with some detail, then expanded into further detail later on throughout ensuing chapters of the book. Sportscasting interest is found everywhere. There are always people who want to dabble in it, like stand-up comedy, even if they aren't really that good at it. They have an opinion, they have the gift of gab, and they want to talk about sports. But there are three categories of interest when it comes to someone's ability to become a sportscaster; hobby, employee or independent contractor.

Hobby – Sportscasting does not have to be a full-time gig. It can be something that you do, regardless of pay, because you enjoy it. But if you do enjoy it, even as a hobby, you should be willing to work on your craft in order to improve it to a top-notch level. The great thing about a hobby is that you aren't focused on getting paid, therefore theoretically, you may find it easier to get involved. Local recreation teams and summer league squads are the best avenue to get a play-by-play hobbyist gig with. They won't pay you, likely not even in food, but they are usually open to having someone do some type of play-by-play for them, as long as you aren't annoying and don't tend to be more trouble than you are worth. Take a handheld recorder along (or a smart phone), do a little prep before the game, and go to town on your new hobby. The only factor is that they likely won't help you with sponsorship to cover costs for food, travel and whatever internet service requirements such as cellular hotspot fees, that you incur on your new hobby. But its commendable if that's how you want to hone

3

your talent into a skill.

It is difficult to deride a hobbyist. They are people who have lives which cannot be broken up by pursuing a full-time career in sportscasting. They have spouses, children, mortgages, a decent or successful career in another industry, and are tied to the local area. And they still love sportscasting. They just don't want to be divorced with their kids taken away from them, lose their income by their steady job evaporating and they seek to remain relevant in their local area.

Employee – This used to be the top route in order to get into sportscasting. Back when each radio station hired on-air talent who would also do sportscasting gigs. It was actually a requirement of radio stations that on-air talent, who were playing music or doing news reports during the week, would be required to spend their nights each weekend doing high school or college play-by-play gigs. Back then, play-by-play announcers were also employees of college athletic departments, high school coaches and minor league teams as well. They had travel paid for, per diems of $50 per game (this has actually gone down since 2008 to this edition's 2020 writing), and put up with a lot of input from people who really don't know sportscasting – namely athletic directors, sports information directors, and parents of the players. Minor league teams may have you as a Director of Broadcasting, as well as selling tickets with a bonus system attached to it.

The benefits were a low risk situation, where as long as you didn't cuss on the air, even if the broadcasting equipment broke, you weren't fired. You'd have a way to list a professional name on your resume, which was on paper not LinkedIn, and you could send out an aircheck via cassette or CD to competing radio stations for better employment. Those days are gone now. Most of those jobs no longer exist. The salad days of the no-risk play-by-play gig has been cut, along with everything else deemed extraneous by college athletics and professional

4

sports teams altogether. Radio and televisions have also followed suit. Namely because they have switched to an independent contractor model, putting the risk right into the lap of the play-by-play announcer.

Independent Contractor – this is the future of sportscasting. It involves the most risk, requiring a lot of hustle, but is also the model of sports play-by-play as everyone across the board looks to cut costs. Radio and televisions stations don't have the ability to pay for overhead expenses such as health benefits, full time salary and travel expenses. Neither do minor league teams or college athletics. While this may seem like a dour note, is actually opens up a lot of possibilities. Instead of being locked into one team, you can build your social media and online following, capture a lot of different sponsors, and increase your overall income simply because your competition has narrowed. The majority of your potential competitors will be turned off by the idea of risk, becoming adverse to making the attempt at an independent contractor-style career in sportscasting. This creates more opportunity for you.

You are the sole point of contact in this scenario. The buck stops with you. That means that you setup the broadcast. You control the online portal and social media accounts, creating the method in (internet livestream / radio / social media) in which the game is broadcast. You do all of the heavy-lifting. If there is a website, you are the one controlling and funding it. If you want to get paid, you hunt down the sponsorship opportunities by making the connections with the local companies interested in doing it. However, that means you also get to have a greater chunk of whatever comes out of the sponsorship, entirely. If you can't make a game, you don't get paid.

Although some people dream of doing this, the actuality of how much work for little pay hits as the reality of time commitment and effort take hold. For every 30 second sponsor advertising on your broadcast, expect about 50-60 hours worth of work to solicit them.

This does not include the 100-200 hours of people saying that they are not interested or that they do not have it in the budget to sponsor your broadcast right now.

This is a dream job for a lot of people, but once the reality hits of actually fighting for it, the majority will back out away. Why? Because there is risk involved. People come into the sports media world thinking that there is money in it, waiting for them. What awaits them is actually a line of people, a massively long line, and the only thing that separates those who work in sports media from those who do not is the amount of risk that they are willing to take on. If you are willing to take on more risk, you will assume more reward. I used to think that independent contractor models were not the norm, but times have changed. And with the higher risk comes the greater reward: A job in sportscasting.

There are other things to consider when going into sportscasting:

Versatility – often sportscasters attempt to call only one sports. Usually a sport that they personally love. Because they "know" that game. Football. Baseball. Hockey. It creates a stale environment for the sportscaster, because they tend to not grow and learn, figuring out new methodology in which to call a sport that is foreign to their personal viewing habits. A challenge to any credible sportscaster is to call a sport that they are somewhat unfamiliar with, or one that they personally can't stand and would not normally sit to watch for pleasure. That challenge teaches them to hone in on different points of action, describing volleyball, tennis or golf differently because they have to consistently keep up with what is going on. The old war-story language in a slow baseball game doesn't work with the speed of a mixed martial arts competition. The goal of sportscasting is to guide the listener through various feelings while presenting a combination of information and poetry when describing the overall product of play.

That doesn't happen if you end up missing fine details that you take for granted, because it feels acceptable to "phone it in" as you've seen that play or game a thousand times. A sportscaster's versatility is about using fresh eyes to convey verbally what they are witnessing to their audience, who may be watching the same play themselves on a video livestream, but requires it be broken down as well by an unbiased witness through their speakers.

Being A Salesperson – Face it. Regardless of why you've wanted to be in sportscasting, you are a sales person. You are selling something. You are constantly selling statistics, information, player/coach biographies and the poetry of the game. You are dipping into every listener's conscience, selling them on why they should continue to view or listen. You need to keep them interested enough not to tune you out completely, so that they either make it through to the commercial breaks (in audio/tv form) or so that they digest the corporate sponsorship information being placed in front of them. Could be signage or other imagery, but its there for a reason. Corporate sponsors need customers to purchase their products. They don't just pay big money for advertising space on the sole benefit of a charitable cause when it comes to sportscasting. You may find certain beneficators who do this; someone with a car dealership whose kid or nephew/niece is on the team, but that revenue won't last long. It is temporary. So it is important that you sell the product being sponsored thoroughly or you won't be successful on-air. Worse yet, you will sound bad off-air when you are speaking to a prospective sponsor about providing you the dollars that you need in order to have your broadcast.

Preparation + Hard Work = Luck – A lot of people will view anything that you do successfully as luck. Mainly because they will not see the preparation that it takes to achieve it. That hard work will pay off if you are consistent and persistent toward making yourself better at your craft. In future chapters, the term "showprep" will be discussed. Let that sink in now. Showprep is about ensuring that you do not take your craft lightly. Even a hobbyist should attempt to generate some showprep. Don't think that you can just jump on a hot microphone, "wing it," and everything will be great. There have been seasoned sportscasters who have lost their jobs by not showprepping and saying whatever comes to mind. Generally, what they end up saying tends to not be well-thought out, offends someone who uses social media to get them fired. This is a tight-rope job, where if you aren't careful, you will lose everything as more people start to listen to your broadcasts.

"Winging it" makes for bad broadcasting anyway. Those who "wing it" tend to fumble around on-air, scrambling for last minute respites of information, confused while the action keeps rolling. Once that game starts, no one is going to stop on the field or court play for the sake of the play-by-play announcer. And a sportscaster who thinks its too much work to prepare ahead of time for their broadcast isn't ready for prime time anyway. Just because you can fool your spouse, parents or friends by sounding like crap doesn't mean you are sounding "awesome" to a viewer or listener who doesn't know or care about you personally. Basically, if you sound like crap, and you cocoon yourself by only caring what your loved ones have to say about your broadcast, you are a fool and no one has the heart to tell you otherwise. Prepare at least 5-6 hours per every hour of broadcasting. Showprep will be covered in a future chapter, and it never hurts to have more information, rather than less, when going into a live-action sportscasting situation.

Criticism – Your parents, spouse and friends are not going to be the audience who will tell you the truth about your sportscasting skills. When you stink, they won't tell you that. They won't want to hurt you, rip your heart out and make you cry. Criticism is hard to come by when you have people who care about you. Neither is reading trollish statements by some jerk who is more angry that you are achieving something that he/she dreams about doing such as sportscasting, but hasn't. Find someone who is disinterested in sports overall, or who has zero interest in telling you that you're either "the greatest sportscaster ever" or the "worst play-by-play person" that they've ever heard. Find someone who is middle of the road, but wants to help you improve. Give them $20 to tell you everything that they feel is wrong with the broadcast. Trust me, they will do it, and not for the $20. They will do it because you are showing respect for their opinion. Don't attempt to "defend yourself" or get angry with what they have to say. Just take the load of constructive criticism, jot down notes and work on how to improve at your craft. Honesty sucks, seriously, but it helps more than it hurts if you know what to do to get better.

Sportscasting Platforms – Congratulations, you are in the one business which is constantly changing. Back in 2008, when I wrote *The Sportscaster's Notebook*, the biggest thing on the block was satellite radio. Internet audio streams were starting to move forward. YouTube was still trying to find its footing because it hadn't been sold to Google yet, and no one actually sponsored Internet radio stations or sportscasts. I recalled at Seattle University from 2006-08, arguing with the men's basketball coach about having an internet radio broadcast. He was so adamant about traditional radio (also known as terrestrial radio), that he got sponsors to pay for time on a local radio station's HD station. We still broadcast it on internet radio, and could show credible listener numbers, while the HD station never had one person even call in to chat during his post-game show. The internet used to be a joke, something that people never understood how to broadcast good audio on. Now, great video is starting to become very viable. Enough to where Vimeo and Youtube are big players, along with Twitch and other Open Broadcast Software (OBS) are bigger players than even some of the traditional television stations.

THE SPORTSCASTER'S NOTEBOOK

Negativity Toward Internet Broadcasts – For most independent contractors, purchasing time on a terrestrial local radio station has been a way to negate the suggestion that the internet is a focusable product and not made for "passive people." This trend started to change about 2012-2013, when older adults, who are the ones making sponsorship buys for companies, joined Facebook and other social media platforms. Basically, the old theory arrives at the thought that no one will pass a dial, stop accidentally, finding the game on your site and stay tuned. Since Facebook's dominance took over, now in 2020s, reaching a massive audience is easier than ever. Especially with livestreaming sporting events, which "feed hop" as Facebook analytics tries to generate more viewership to keep people entertained on the platform. The great part about Internet broadcasts is that you can show actual numbers. You can show demographics. And you can present eyeballs for advertisers, who may not get the same reach as they might with small market terrestrial radio stations.

Buying Time On Radio Stations – This used to be the model of independent contractors. Purchasing chunks of radio time to do sportscasting of local games. Three hour blocks purchased for $500, then resold into smaller ads within the sportscasting. Traditional radio stations no longer have the clout anymore to sustain this type of block buying of time. Fewer people listen to the radio, and will easily look at social media broadcasts, which they can play on their smart phones while driving down the street. The only reasoning behind purchasing blocks of time is to grab local sponsors who are also advertising on the radio station otherwise, because it allows the sportscaster credibility with their broadcast. But overall, it is not a good business model for sportscasters anymore as social media can provide more eyeballs, and more advertisers are seeing those digital platforms as credible as they would traditional media like television, newspaper or radio.

TROY KIRBY

EXPECTATIONS AS A SPORTSCASTER

Expect a sportscasting career requires long hours, and you may have nothing to show for it but some mp3 recordings of your play-by-play and a couple hundred dollars missing from your wallet.

Expect that your spouse or significant other will not understand why you are stupid enough to keep doing this.

Expect to miss dinners as well as other appointments, because you are working at a job that pays nothing or next to nothing.

Expect to lose money if you attempt to buy time and sell sponsorship itself, unless you decide to take it truly seriously or start months ahead of the sports season.

Expect that your boss at your real job won't understand why you are doing what you do.

Expect people to suggest that you would be further ahead in your traditional career (job promotions, salary, etc) if you didn't devote your time toward sportscasting.

Expect to live or die with a team that you are sportscasting for, especially when it is a girls/women's team, and they lose (mainly because the players tend to be nicer due to a lack of media attention, and don't deserve to face such heartache. Trust me, it will kill you when they lose).

Expect to have a fulfilling time doing something that other people don't understand.

THE SPORTSCASTER'S NOTEBOOK

Expect to have mean trolls who wish to take you down with snide remarks online due to unprofessional jealousy.

Expect your loved ones to seriously wish you would quit sportscasting because of the time commitment involved, and secretly or publicly voice their opinion.

Expect that what you will experience is the goal of being passionate and crazy toward an ideal that few people will understand, mainly because they cannot comprehend attempting such a risky endeavor as they get older. You are one of the lucky ones who gets to live out their dreams of sportscasting while the rest sit frustrated, watching the clock at work until it is time to go home and retire… Congrats.

Chapter Two

Finding Your Target Market

Defining a target market is a key principle of any business. That includes the world of sportscasting. How you position yourself as a sportscaster matters. Especially when you are not speaking entirely to your target market in general. When you neglect your target market, you actually eliminate listeners and lose money for either the radio station, or yourself. Podcasting has become a niche way of learning who your target market is. You can hone in directly on a market, because the downloads tell you where the listeners are from and what they are interested in listening to.

For instance, what if you decide to solicit sponsorship by expensive vacation resorts or luxury automobiles during a high school basketball tournament?

What if the primary audience listening to that tournament is comprised of low income families in small residential neighborhoods? You would likely miss your target audience and your sponsors would not sell anything because of it. Thus, a lose-lose situation exists.

Sponsors need to see real dollars coming back through their doors when they are making financial decisions. The reality is that if you do not help them earn new customers or business, they will not sponsor you a second time around, and word will get out to other sponsors, losing you more business in the long run.

The first thing that you need to do is pinpoint your target market by seeing who in the market you want to target.

Let's say that you are attempting to focus on a college basketball target market: Which means **men, ages 35-65**.

TROY KIRBY

TARGET: Middle class families

SPONSORS: Real estate, banks, exercise gyms, dentists, hair dressers, clothing stores, fast food and restaurants.

TARGET: Men (ages 25-35)

SPONSORS: Electronics, video games, potato chips, cars, casinos, movies, coffee and alcohol.

TARGET: Men (ages 55-65)

SPONSORS: Luxury automotive, vacations, retirement communities, condos, golf course, insurance, doctors, lawyers.

Notice how each sponsor has its own target demographic that it is trying to reach. This is due to the **55-65 year old men** who are interested in condos being disinterested in real estate as much as middle class families might because middle class families want to move into a bigger home from their current one. And while middle class families may be interested in advertisements about restaurants, they may not be as interested in alcohol advertisements as **men ages 25-35**.

This does not mean that you cannot have a sponsor which favors one target market over the other. However, if none of the sponsors that you have are appealing to at least one of the target markets that you have, it is a wasted effort to attempt to solicit sponsorship from that sponsor. If you have a mutual funds sponsor, but that appeals to **men ages 45-55** and they do not listen to your broadcast in enough numbers that matter, then you wasted that sponsor's time and resource. And the listener hears an advertisement that doesn't concern them, which feels like dead air.

Chapter Three

One or Two Person Crew

There are specific roles and duties for a sportscasting duo. They are doled out in regards to a two-person crew, with the ability for each person to shine at their specific roles. But each person has to stay within their lane in order for the entire operation to work. Keep in mind, the listener needs balance, harmony, to be able to truly enough the product that you are putting into their ears. When a sportscasting team does not find its rhythm, when it instead has two people trying to compete for time, talking over each other, not playing well in the sandbox together, it is the listener who receives the failed product.

If you are going to do your broadcasts solo, which many of you are, some of these details are still good to review. Basically, the first rule of sportscasting in regards to a two-man operation is to allow the listener to understand what is going on. The action on the field or court matters. Description. Ease. Entertainment. This means that you as the sportscaster are providing a steady stream of good information with a blend of both voices, when you are in a two-person crew. Even if you cannot stand the other person in every other setting, when the microphone is "hot," both of you must act as a tandem to other, providing as much description, information and insight so that the listener receives the best broadcast possible. Otherwise, you have failed the listener, and your team is a failure overall.

Personalities conflict. People argue, they fight, they do not get along. Sometimes, they outright despise each other for personal or professional reasons. But when you are working with someone else on air during a sportscast, you need to be in sync. You need to have the best interests of the sports fan listening, not yourself, in mind. There will be situations where the color announcer will end up talking more than the play-by-play announcer. Or where the play-by-play announcer has to really detail out an entire situation, and the color announcer needs to sit back, without saying much, and let the game play out. Both announcers are leaving their egos at the door, allowing the listener to gain the value of what matters most; the best broadcast of the game.

Typically, egos are fashioned based off of a lack of preparation and trust with each other. That comes from one of the crew showing up only two minutes before air time. They give off a sense that they don't respect the time of the person that they are doing the sportscast with. A lot of people who think that sportscasting is easy tend to not value the time put in as a professional broadcaster. Or they believe that they can do the sportscast without the other person there. It is important that the play by play announcer and the color announcer realize the value in the other, as it presents a greater broadcast overall for the viewer, who know gets to learn more about the facets of the game that they are watching or listening to.

When a person shows up 10 minutes prior to the game without any show prep, or expects that the prep will be built for them, then the broadcast suffers. As does the other member of the two-person crew, who showed up ahead of time, did their show prep by talking to players and coaches in order to get names correctly pronounced, learn tidbits about what was happening during the week, etc. All of that goes into the sportscast. And when a one person on a two-person crew doesn't show value to their partner, the entire operation suffers as a result.

As mentioned in the previous chapter and in other chapters ahead, you should prep 5-6 hours per 1 hour of broadcasting. That's because you need to get detailed information on both teams, as well as make a few phone calls/send emails to visiting coaches/players, etc in order to build out the best broadcast possible. When you fail to really put the time in, you are showing every audience member that they can put a tape in, call up the radio station and do play by play of the game.

Essentially, a talentless situation where anybody could do sportscasting. That's not the case, and the line of demarcation is your showprep. If you deliver on showprep, you will wow anyone viewing or listening with the amount of knowledge that you have to offer your sportscast.

A lot of people are shocked to see the 5-6 hours of show prep per 1 hour of broadcasting rule. That estimation is on the low end, if you really want to do an incredible sportscast. Understand that this is your increased value to the entire presentation. That when you get the visiting coach on the phone and you talk for two hours, learning all of the details of their season, past opponents, etc., it blends in with what you know about the hometown team that you usually cover. When you can chat up an opposing player or two, then coupled with heading the home team practices, getting notes and information on what's happened with the players and coaches, this builds out your entire sportscast. You are the outlet for both teams to talk to their fans, and know exactly what information is of interest, especially during the dull parts of the game.

This only intensifies when you are talking about a two-person crew. Both will come from different lines of thinking – a color announcer typically is a former player or coach, who has a deeper playing knowledge to deliver to the audience. When you also arrange conversations off-air where the play-by-play announcer and color announcer can work together, prepare their show, it creates a passionate blend of good information from voices and opinions that needs to go on during the entire broadcast.

Historically, men have felt some discomfort staring at each other. However, this is a big part of sportscasting when working in a two-person operation. There needs to be a set of non-verbal cues which occur, mainly staring at your partner while they are talking, to know when they are finished with a sentence and when you can begin to speak. Both of announcers in a two-person crew should work on allowing two-second breaths between one announcer ending their statement and the other announcer beginning theirs. This is not a competition for air time. Nor is it a good idea to start contradicting each other, and making one of you look bad. This is about providing non-verbal cues instead of verbal ones like "let me finish" statements that end up harming the sportscast and allowing the entire team to sound weak.

The play-by-play announcer and the color announcer have specific, set duties on how they should carry themselves on the sportscast. It is up to both members of the two-person crew to highlight and understand what they can, and what they cannot, be responsible for.

TROY KIRBY

Play-By-Play Announcer Duties

- The visual carrier of the mental picture for the viewer/listener of the sportscast. They know the names, scores, times and positions of each player. They understand how to convey each bit of information into a blended listening experience in which audience may tune in, or tune out, of the broadcast, during different periods, but still keeps the audience informed when they do return, as to what is going on in the game.

- Impartial (to a degree) to balance-out the color announcer (analyst) or simply conveys the action on the field or court to the viewer/listener. Doesn't try to out-scream or out-shout anyone. Instead, they are more interested in presenting details, even above the excitement of the action on the field or court.

- Takes primary position while audio broadcasting, takes secondary position on video broadcasting.

- Gives out reminders of score and times constantly on audio, lightly on video where the score/time is visually shown.

- Seemlessly transitions the conversation between the game action over to the color analyst.

- An independent voice, not attempting to give excuses or reasons for why the action is happening, instead focusing on overall game flow. Details are important rather than why the play has developed or was run in the first place.

- Tries to be the voice of reason while sitting with the color analyst, but uses open-ended questioning to the color analyst in order to lead the color analyst's examination of what is going on in the game further, creating more information, poetry and detail toward situational conflicts on the field or court. The goal is always to help the viewer/listener understand what is happening and why.

TROY KIRBY

Color Analyst/Announcer Duties

- Helps develop the listener's mental picture through verbal cues that enhance the overall sportscast. The color analyst is the strategist of the two-person sportscast.

- Provides sound reasoning behind each offense/defensive play, ruling interpretations on the field or court, and why that method of play calling has been successful or unsuccessful against the opposition.

- Supports why a play occurred and provides predictions as to what future playcalling may occur in order to either correct past bad plays or increase the good plays coming.

- Chief analyst of what the coaches are telling the players during timeouts, and what is being said to correct negative plays of action that have occurred in the game. Color analysts typically showcase their insider knowledge of how the coaching staff and the players interact in the locker room on the sidelines, based on the color analyst's past, personal experience in the same situations (if possible).

- The color analyst is not an independent voice. They support the team affiliated with the sportscast and they attempt to enhance the product of the game through analysis which is accurate and honest.

- Serves as a secondary role on audio, a primary role on video.

- Knows when to shut up and doesn't relate everything back to their own experience wholly. Instead, they attempt to show the commonalities and insight of the game through intense research, personal interviews/conversations with the players and coaching staff, and by developing a strong commentary.

THE SPORTSCASTER'S NOTEBOOK

- The color analyst is not merely a statistics reader. They are there to illustrate a thought process that helps complete the voice of opinion relevant to viewers/listeners who are also doing the same. In a way, the color analyst has to be in sync with the listening/viewing audience in what they want to have explained as part of the process of the game during play and breaks in the action.

TROY KIRBY

Non-Verbal Cues

When you are working with a partner on the air, it is hard to let them know when you are talking and when they are supposed to speak. The art of non-verbal communication is key to developing a good sportscast. Turning and looking at the partner, making eye contact, is the best way to let them know when you are ready to speak. It also allows them to know when they can shut up, etc.

When the player with the ball crosses the half-court line, the play by play announcer **takes over** talking.

When the ball is dropped in the basket, the play by play announcer finishes the play, then **allows** the color analyst to give further description or analysis.

Let the color analyst be the **main interviewer** for halftime guests. Allow the play by play announcer to rest their voice.

The Play-By-Play announcer **should pose leading questions** to the color analyst which allow the color analyst to **open up** about the game action and give it more detail.

Chapter Four

Play-By-Play
and
Social Media

In 2022, as well as beyond, every sports broadcaster has a choice of how they want to initiate their social media and content channels. Several do not understand that this is not the 1970s anymore. You cannot get away with a lack of content. This is what drives listener affinity toward what you do. Now, you have to create a sound social media profile. There needs to be a set business plan on how you want to initiate, as well as continue to produce, your content for individual digital platforms. The more that you sit out, the more that you lose.

This is not about having brash opinions that generate buzz controversy. This is about ensuring that you, the sports broadcaster, are relevant in the new age in several different ways. There are things that you will be required to do that legendary sports broadcasters like Chick Hearn didn't have to do while performing play-by-play each night for the Los Angeles Lakers in the 1970s and 1980s. Hearn did have to do on-air interviews by local TV jocks several times a week or other newspaper publication interviews, because that was the media available and that was the job required of him. That's the difference maker. The days of the media coming to you are gone. Now, you are the content, you are the driver, you are the media, you are the platform.

Right now, there are play-by-play announcers who are taking two set paths on social media: Either they have zero or little social media contact / information available for the public to digest or engage with, or they are the meathead in the room – i.e. they say stupid, controversial, divisive crap disguised as "sports opinion" because they demand to drive social media outrage traffic, only to arrive at the day they are forced to "apologize" or risk losing their job because they truly offended enough people with the bile that they put out into the world. Neither of these paths are sustainable long term for the sports broadcaster. Even Howard Cosell found his "third rail" by writing a book in 1985 which criticized his fellow Monday Night Football booth mates – surprisingly, he was not welcomed back into the booth for the following season's games and his career was basically over. And this was before social media. Imagine the issues now with making such a mistake.

The goal should be to think differently by being different. Even if you are in the smallest of towns, you can be the center of the sports world when you broadcast and when you continue to put out content. You are the epicenter of your own sports universe when you focus on the right things that drive interesting, compelling content that people want to digest. Instead of making dumb attempts to outrage people, why not provide extra content on your social media platforms to your listeners? Create context, not controversy. Think about the position that you are in, as a sports broadcaster: You have access, the keys to the castle. You can provide way more insight because you have the ability to produce photos, video, and audio, as well as write compelling insider information, which drives true conversation for your listeners / viewers.

What if you added extra short interviews or off-the-cuff commentary from players / coaches that drove listener content back toward the play-by-play broadcasters? What if you took an additional 10 minutes prior to or after each game, interviewed two people, then put that audio / video up as additional content on your social media platforms? Think about the relevance that you have in creating something unique that only can be accessed by listeners / viewers who subscribe to your blog or website. This is how you create further interest, along with a tribe of folks who are tuned into what you specifically have to offer. Because it is unique and found nowhere else except on your digital platforms. This is how you win at this game.

What do I mean by that? There is a secondary game being played beyond the one on the court. You are essentially a platform. A brand. You have to admit that you are an access point to those who wish they could have your job. So you have to continually earn that position. That means that you have to amplify anything around you, to showcase that you are in a place where you have access to information, visual or audio, that others are interested in. Walking through the arena or ballpark, it is important to see that you can sustain more power than those around you. This doesn't have to contain mere interviews with players on the court either. This could be an access point to fans of the game interviews. Or an interest piece focused on one of the game staff. Or the building itself.

What you should be doing is trying to provide what matters. You need the listener / viewer to see this as a window into a world that they wish to belong. A place that you actually are living in constantly. This is about fear of missing out by your fans. They yearn for the ability to get behind the scenes details that are beyond the scores themselves. You could also hype up those extra bits of content during the game. This tells your listeners / viewers that they have an access point to find additional information of entertainment to digest. Once they arrive at your social media platforms, they become part of your tribe. It is strongly suggested that you do your platforms differently as well. Understand how each platform engages, and to whom each platform speaks to. Not every platform is the same or has a similar audience. Creating a domain name specific to your brand also allows you to collect email addresses as well as other information.

Example: Dan Harrington has www.danstakes.com and has given away team jerseys, tickets, and other items on his site. He also has links to all of his social media, an email address collector, and expanded blog takes. There are ways to like and subscribe to different content. Every day, he posts something new. It might be an audio interview or some of form of content, but it is there.

This leads into the idea of scheduling content out weeks in advance if possible. When you do this, adding in timely bits of information when they occur, it creates greater headway for both the breaking news as well as the additional content overall. Imagine creating a checklist of things that you have to do, getting several different pieces of content more than 3-4 weeks in advance, then scheduling it out. Ensuring that everything is ready, always deliverable, etc. This is done by creating a content calendar of information. If you gathered about 20 minutes of a player interview, but separated it into 2-3 segments, that's additional content spread out over the course of a few days or weeks. Think about the largess of that ability to engross people with new scheduled content, coupled around breaking news. It makes you, the announcer, a media source that fans continue to focus on.

Social Media Checklist
☒ Instagram Photo
☒ Podcast Audio Clip
☒ 2 Minute Facebook LIVE Video
☒ 2 Twitter LIVE Video
☒ TikTok Video

Specialized Giveaways - You also have the ability to do specialized giveaway contests to your tribe. Think about how the teams that you are covering do merchandise or tickets. They might provide you extra swag or free tickets as a bonus to doing the games. So imagine that you run online digital contests for your listeners who write up Google Reviews or other flattering ways to promote your social media brand. Maybe a "commenter" of the post. And then you select that winner, pop the item in the mail to them, and they feel rewarded. You might even do up your own t-shirts or buttons, anything which pushes the narrative that these are your followers. This creates an affinity toward you and helps you in the long run when there are promotions to other stations or other avenues to be a part of the overall structure. People with fans attached to them can bring in listeners as well as numbers. Where there are people, there is power.

This extends further by allowing the play-by-play announcer to push out breaking news. The PBP often hears information before anyone else, including the rest of the media. Work out a system with the PR director of the team to ensure that it is information that they want out there. Then break the news first, asking for a 20-30 minute buffer between that information being released to the rest of the media. Think about not only injuries, but signings of new players, or other important information. It allows the team to know that they can drive traffic as well as attention through your brand and social media channels.

Membership model – There are platforms such as Patreon which allow you to blog, provide podcasts, videocasts and have folks pay a subscription fee to view it. This is a great way to allow people to see behind the curtain and for it to be additionally profitable to you as a play-by-play announcer. This is where you can chat about additional calls, plays, or have those extra interviews with players/coaches about a specific game. Maybe even do highlighted action as well as extra insight. This is the wave of the future for the PBP announcer. Radio stations especially require more content than ever, even if it cannot go on their actual airwaves. This also allows for podcasting opportunities of interviews that had to be cut down to fit a 30-minute window that ran longer, and it allows for other journalists to be interviewed by the PBP announcer, thus bringing in an additional audience while protecting the content.

Avoiding the Trolls – The idea that you have to engage with everyone is silly. If someone is being a sullen jerk, it is best to ignore them. If they continue their remarks, then bounce them from the social media platform or ban them. Especially if they are attacking other social media followers on your page.

Chapter Five

Advice
for
Play-by-Play Announcers

The play-by-play (PBP) has a dual role in most of the sportscasting that they will do. Namely because they have to provide everything on a solo basis. Color analysts are usually not a part of road work, even if its 30 miles from the home team's confines to an away opponent. It means that the PBP has to be ready, willing and able to establish as much of the same environment as a two-person crew would provide. The PBP is usually solo on a high school or small college sportscast. The big budgets of having a color analyst or sideline reporter are when a broadcast trailer is parked behind the stadium. Mainly because compensation for broadcasts is not what it used to be.

At other times, when the PBP can find someone else to join the broadcast as uncompensated addition, it is a struggle to create a new system of non-verbal cues, attempting to find a harmony and sync with a partner who is not paid to be there, thus unlikely to take it seriously enough to show prep the required 5-6 hours per 1 hour of broadcasting formula described in previous chapters.

Breakdown of 7:05 p.m. tip-off basketball game
6:00 a.m. - 1-2 hours show prep before work: past highlights / game focus.
7:45 a.m. - Make sure all play-by-play equipment is packed in car trunk.
10:00 a.m. - At job site, 15 minute break focus: one-liner game calls.
12:00 p.m. - 1 hour lunch break focus: show prep of coaches, players, stats
3:30 p.m. - At job site, 15 minute break focus: Player pronunciations.
5:00 p.m. - Leave job site, drive to venue, focus: Do calls mentally & prep.
5:30 p.m. - At venue, find game table seat assignment, set up equipment, test.
5:45 p.m. - Get rosters, find who is on, who is off, what is needed.
5:55 p.m. - Chat up players, ensure name pronunciations. Get tidbits, details.
6:10 p.m. - Start boot camp with show prep, put in the extra work.
6:45 p.m. - Sit at game table assignment, chat up refs, scorekeepers, etc.
6:55 p.m. - Do final test of equipment. Go LIVE and start broadcast at 7:00 p.m.
7:05 p.m. - Tip-off begins.

THE SPORTSCASTER'S NOTEBOOK

This means that the PBP has to really take it upon themselves to show the overall value of making a solo announcing gig sound as if it has a large amount of value embedded within the entire sportscast.

Actor Tom Skerritt (Picket Fences, Alien) teaches a film class in Seattle, Washington without the use of cameras. This is a foreign concept to most film departments on a college campus. Namely because the first thing that college campus film departments do is hand their students a camera and tell them to go shoot film. Skerritt does the opposite, for good reason. His theory is a sound one, that camera work is a component of filmmaking, but never the main artery of the entire ecosystem. If you simply film without having a script, then you are hoping for something good to happen with little to no recourse if it doesn't happen. You have a bunch of wasted footage.

Skerrit's classes teach screenwriting mainly; how to develop more of your characters, of your scenes, and how to show that writing visually in front of a camera lens, ensuring that the dead eye of the camera will pick it up. The same is true for the sportscasting performed along with this book. Too often, we have people willing to talk in front of a "hot mic" situation, rambling about the game in front of them. Very little detail, no harmony of sync. Essentially, they are victims of a lack of show prep. Where they call it as they see it, which is both uninteresting and alludes to the notion that anyone can do a sportscasting job. If you do not take the time to prepare to make yourself great at your craft, you will sound like everyone else, which isn't very flattering if you think about it.

Start tossing those bad special phrases that you came up with. That "catch phrase" or "cliché" isn't worth it and a waste of breath on a hot mic during a game. It also won't come out during the right time, will sound silly, and will end up being something that viewers/listeners mock more than celebrate. Those garbage lines are meant to distract, not there to enhance, the way that people gain a mental picture from a verbal cue. Your broadcasts need to bring them in, not make them shake their head and ignore it as "cheesy." Focus on the poetry of the game, how it is flowing, and the harmonious ways that it gradually builds to a greater conclusion. Understand the each essence of how the play is formed on the court or field is different from how the viewer/listener conceives it. That is why you are there, to enhance the overall broadcast through your presentation of description.

Keep in mind that you need to "set-up" the action as much as you call it. This means knowing more about the plays and sport in advance of the specific game that you are calling. Frequently, inexperienced PBP will be the flow of the game determined by the ball involved, which makes it sound like a dull second day of the NFL Draft – 2-3 hours of calling names without much to react to. This exposes a lack of show prep, which also means learning about the game, watching past videos of other broadcasts to get the nuances involved, and understanding that you are supposed to enhance the overall package for the viewer/listener, not merely serve as a placeholding announcer.

A great PBP will focus on "blending" the broadcast by giving some details as well as what might happen, who is open to progress the offense, who is being looked to prevent that offense through defense, what play is being set and who is coming into the game. This type of "blended" broadcast will create a mental picture from your verbal cues, allowing the listener/viewer to feel as if the broadcast is enhanced by what you say, and by you being a part of it. There is a part of showprep which speaks to knowing more about what not to say, then what to say, which increases the overall sportscasting package as well.

The PBP uses their eyes to describe each play's design and breakdown. But, exactly how does someone do that? Try looking up different games on YouTube or borrow game film from a coach or friend. Every coach has a ton of game film on their own home/away games, and if they understand why you need to borrow it, they are likely to give you a copy or two on a thumbdrive. The film needs to be continuous however, without different camera breaks. This needs to be side to side panning, as you would watch a game from the press box, so that you can understand and grasp the complexity, as well as the simplistic nature, of how to sportscast a game. Whether that be football, basketball, baseball or even the drone racing league. You need to be able to have a consistent flow, in order to move forward with your broadcasting skills.

NOTE: Don't worry about reading the numbers or always announcing the score when using game film to build your PBP. This is about creating your skillset. Use generic names, and be patient, as this is a learning experience. You will probably need to call about 4-5 games off of YouTube – do the entire match/game from end to end, without stopping. This is how you can properly prepare to call a live action game. Everyone is different. Never practice call off of the same YouTube footage twice, since during your entire sportscasting career, it will be built off of spontaneous calls.

Here are a series of five developed methods to help anyone improve their **PBP** skills.

Method #1

Know the dimensions of the court.

High school court – 84 ft x 50 ft

College/pro court – 94 ft x 50 ft

Baseline to free throw line -19 ft

Width of the lane - 12 ft

Free throw line to backboard – 15 ft

College/High School 3pt line – 19.75 ft

Pro 3pt line – 23.75 ft

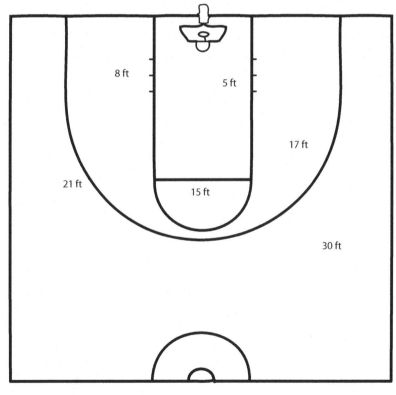

THE SPORTSCASTER'S NOTEBOOK

Method #2

Describe the shot and the shooter:

1. Area on the court where the player took the shot. Example: *"Bobby off the left wing with the shot."*

2. Where did the ball land it did not go in the basket. Example: *"Ball pops up off of the left hand side of the rim and goes out of bounds."*

3. Did the ball hit the backboard? Example: *"The ball hits the top of the backboard's box and rims off down the left side."*

4. Did the ball hit above, to a side or inside the backboard's box?

5. If the ball landed out of bounds – describe the baseline (are there letters spelling out the team's name? If so, on which letters did it land?) Example: *"Garrings' shot lands out of bounds, hitting near the A-L of the word FALCONS written across the baseline of the court."*

basketball backboard

left	top
outside box	
inside box	
bottom	right

6. Did the ball land near one of the corners or near a fan?

   a. What did the fan look like?

   b. Where the cheerleaders nearby?

7. What if the shooter off-balance? **Example:** "*Simmons tosses up an awkward shot toward the basket with her right hand and twists like a pretzel.*"

8. Did the shooter fall away or get pushed away after the shot? **Example:** "*Leslie gets hammered by two defenders after the shot is put up.*"

9. How did the shooter land (on his back or stomach)? **Example:** "*Herr does a belly flop on the box.*"

10. Was it an open shot or did the shooter have someone guarding him? **Example:** "*Yancy, double-teamed, still finds a way to get to the hole.*"

11. How did the shooter get off the shot while being guarded (a juke move?)? **Example:** "*Jamal gets juked out of his shoes by Stevens who throws up a prayer.*"

THE SPORTSCASTER'S NOTEBOOK

Method #3

Break down the field of play into different segments:

The diagram below features a lot of different terms for the half court.

This is to help you blend in a broadcast with more description and allow the listener not to feel they are being fed repetitive lines.

The last thing that a sportscaster wants to do is bore an audience, because they usually tune out.

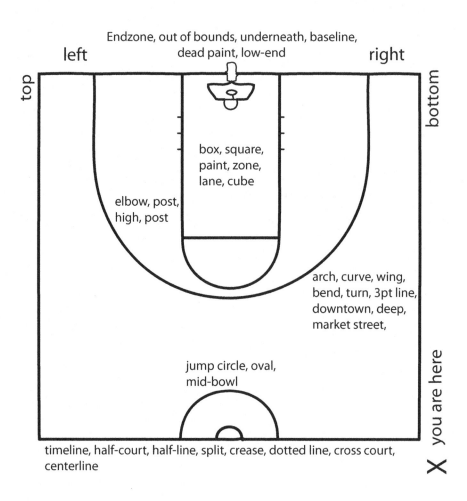

Method #4

Using game tapes borrowed from a friend or coach or by grabbing them off of YouTube, I would suggest calling at least 3-5 plays of each of the following to create good theater and build-up for action as the listener is given an enhanced version of your sportscast.

1. Focus on a player who does not have the ball. Where are they on the floor? What are they doing without the ball? Who is defending them/who are they defending? **Example:** *"Rider is being blocked out on the low end with his hands up, waiting for the pass inside the left end of the box as Stevens circles the arch with the ball."*

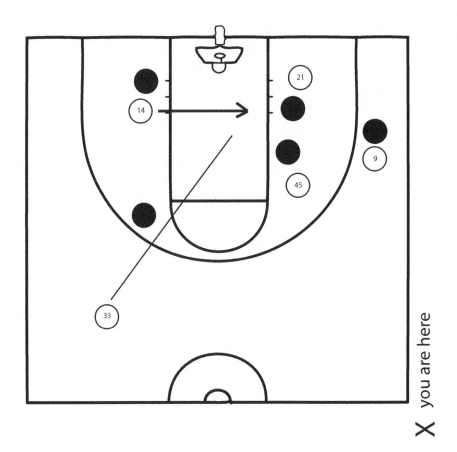

2. Talk about the entire defense being carried by out the team. What defense are they playing? Who is playing out of position? Who is being double-teamed? Triple-teamed? Who is quicker than their opponent? Slower? **Example:** *"The Wave drop back into a 3-2 zone with Henderson hiding on the right end of the box, working past the screen of Dearborn as Garrison's point guard is being trapped over on the top right corner."*

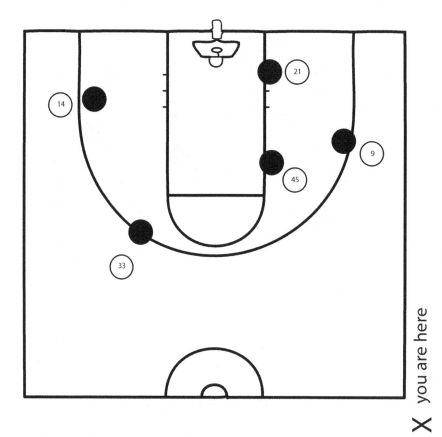

3. The entire offense being carried out by a team? What offense are they playing? Are they driving forward or being pushed back? Are they passing the ball or keeping it to one side of the court? Is one player acting as a leader or are all of the players talking to each other? **Example:** *"Crossing half-court, Jamison with the ball uses his right hand to decide a new play, showing three fingers high as the 2-1-2 zone applies too much pressure for the Devils do anything inside."*

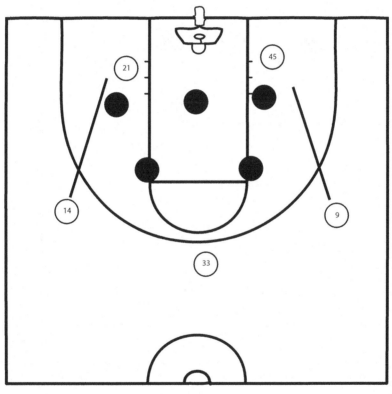

4. Name the actions of every player on the court without the ball. Anytime they receive the ball, talk about everyone but them.
    Example: *"Henry keeps his defender behind him, waving his arms for the ball, then slips around the defender as the pass goes high his way."*

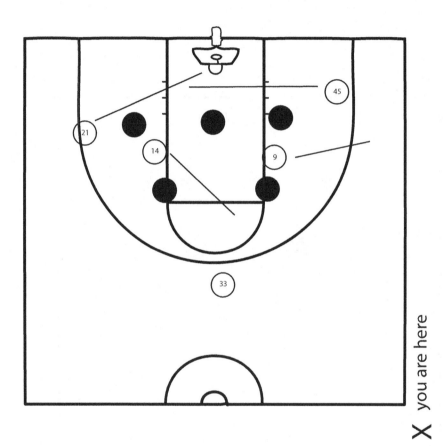

5. **Talk about how the player dribbles the ball:** Is it between their legs? With a stutter step as if to drive to the basket? With a fake pass to the right, then a real pass to the left? **Example:** *"Wills uses the crossover to move pass Derring and shifts off to the left side of the post, chest pass to Franklin all alone for the dunk."*

6. **Talk about how a person passes the ball:** Do they pass from the chest? Do they pass using both hands? Just the right or left? **Example:** *"Fewing does a back turn to his right, bounces the ball off the court and into the hands of Derek who flips one over his defender right to Browning for the dunk."*

7. **Talk about what is the coach doing and follow the actions of the coaching staff:** Are they agitated or calm? Are they making quick substitutions or merely responding to situations in the game? Are the players responding to the coaches, or ignoring them? How is the coach reacting the officiating? How is the coach reacting to a play that goes their way? How is the coach responding to a broken play? Is the coach standing in one place or walking the sideline? Describe what the coach is wearing, whether they are kneeling or standing, or sitting during the game. Do they shout plays or do they make hand gestures or do they cover their mouths with clip boards? **Example:** *"Coach Reed is hot under the collar after watching that dunk and turns to make sure the players on the bench know what went wrong with that defense."*

8. **Call the crowd:** Give in detail what the crowd is doing and why they are doing it? Are they shouting, booing, crying, sneezing? Is it a zoo or are they quiet? **Example:** *"Probably one of the loudest school bands ever is playing tonight, blasting away as the students rock this joint silly after that dunk by Virgil to take a 10 point lead over St. Mary's."*

9. **Look at the building:** What about it is unique, what does the scoreboard look like? Is the ceiling low, are the lights bright or dim? Is there a blockade of signs (boosters, sponsors, etc) or is it vacant? **Example:** *"The Wooden Cage has been around since the 50s, if you can hear an annoying creaking sound in this broadcast, that's because they still have the same bleachers in place from the day they built it."*

Method #5

More ways using YouTube game footage. Here are some tips to ensure that as you advance, you are creating muscle memory techniques will stay with you forever.

1. **Call the game wrong;** take a basketball game and only use soccer terminology. Use a baseball game and only broadcast as if you are sportscasting a football game. What this will do is show you how rushed you sounded in certain situations, where it is not necessary. You want to build up a consistent pace, but also understand that you are engaging your audience in a wholly dynamic way. If you call a game wrong intentionally and it doesn't sound wrong, then you don't know the game well enough to screw it up.

2. **Log onto Twitch, which is game site, and attempt to call one of their eSports games while others play.** You will be able to get the nuances of the game, especially as the camera angles switch on you. This will create an unnerving environment where you learn what the viewer/listener witnesses, and how to ensure that between any video feed cuts, you are delivering a consistent product that the viewer/listener can fully understand.

3. **Call a game only as a color announcer.** Don't do any play by play. See what you miss, and what you add to the game. See how your analysis works, while only providing limited amount of information through what you have to say. Remember, you are providing less in this role if its an audio presentation, and will be talking more if it's a video presentation.

4. **Go to comedy club open mic nights.** Talk to those going up on stage. See how they write, how they think quickly on their feet. They want to enhance what their jokes are, but also feed off of the crowd reaction, especially when hecklers come in. How do they do so but make the entire environment spontaneous? You

might want to consider signing up yourself, tell a few jokes, and see how it feels to be the sole voice in a room, on stage, in front of lights, where the audience is something you can hear, but not see. Very strange, terrifying, but great if you want to learn how to grow as a broadcaster.

5. **Head to several games where you are not broadcasting.** Sit in the stands, but compile as much showprep ahead of time, and take out a handheld recorder (I use a Zoom H4N). Do the entire game, start to finish, using your showprep notes. You may get a few folks interested in what you are doing, but so what? Keep recording, do your recording, then listen to it on your drive home. See whether it conveys enough of the poetry, or if you have to develop more as a sportscaster. This will also serve as a great sample tape for any team that needs a sportscaster for their audio or video livestreaming.

Chapter Six

Exercises
for
Play-by-Play Announcers

The Art of the Over-Smile – Listeners to audio broadcasts do not have the luxury of seeing you smile. Nor do most video broadcasts, where you are not the focal point of attention because the game of play is. That means that if you do not make a drastic attempt to constantly "over-smile" when you broadcast PBP, you will sound monotone and unhappy. The listener picks this up immediately. Part of the art of over-smiling, which has been utilized by everyone from telemarketers to radio broadcasts for over a century, is to stare into the mirror at yourself, and make the attempt to talk. Do it on any bit of script. Keep over-smiling. If your cheekbones aren't showing, then you aren't doing it right. Consider this, that sportscasting is supposed to be a fun, exciting job. That you are supposed to be thrilled to be a part of the action, sportscasting in an environment and vantage point that few others get to be a part of. The listening public needs to feel that you are emotionally part of the sportscast, otherwise you are not a key part of its presentation.

While you are over-smiling, you will see "Joker Face" in the mirror. Because you look like Batman's arch enemy villain. Do it for at least 30-to-45 minutes in one standing. Call out a game. Make up some references. Get yourself used to the idea of carrying those facial muscles in that pattern. Your mouth will ache, especially around the sides, but will grow used to it as you reap the rewards of non-monotone sportscasting. Practicing your over-smile in different situations, such as phone calls, as you speak. The results will be drastic, but don't giggle when you over-smile.

One of the issues that today's youth have is that they don't talk as much in general as past generations as technology has changed. They tend to instant message or text or email. This is not a good thing for a sportscaster, but if you can start talking more, using the telephone more, having your conversations as a face-to-face interaction, you will grow your sportscasting brand. It isn't merely saying a lot of words, but gaining a timed inflection to ensure that you are speaking in an abundant array.

Work On Your Timing – Take a handheld recorder or your smart phone, then read off the following script:

Tonight, the Cyclones take on the Barnstormers in what could be the match-up of the season. Coach Garry Jones for the Cyclones has his team ready, with a 12-5 record midway through the year, while Barnstormers' John O'Jay has his team only one game ahead at 13-4, but has two of his five starters out for the next week with injuries. Will this be the decider for the state championship? Opening tip is only seconds away here on the Inland Sports Radio network after words from our sponsors.

So, how long did it take to voice out? A minute? 45 seconds? 30 seconds? Whatever time it took, I want to you re-voice it and attempt to shave off 5-10 seconds. You must sound coherent, over-smile, but I want you to do it again. Check the time, then do it again. After a bit, you will start to learn how long 15 or 30 seconds is when you voice. Do it several different ways, including fast or slow, happy or sad. Inflect your voice on the coaches names and playing records with emphasis. Then be very pointed on the question mark, take a one second pause, then finish the next sentence.

What you are doing is developing your own timing. You will eventually do this with your own writing. The key is to learn how to take prepared statements, grow them with the power of your voice and initiate a skillset of delivering that to the listeners. Think about your competing sportscasters who are not doing this. Who are not trying their hardest to developing their timing. When you work on your timing, along with your over-smiling, you are creating a sound worth listening to in sportscasting. Keep it up. It is not a skill that you can use then drop or let go lax. You must work at it every day to sound the best to your listener. It separates you from those who do not work as hard.

THE SPORTSCASTER'S NOTEBOOK

Constants – There are specific constants in sportscasting which should be followed. Remember that you are the verbal carrier of the mental picture for every listener. Time, Score, Teams, shot clock (with 9 or less to go), player fouls, team fouls, where are the teams are playing, timeouts each team has. This is especially true of time and score. Those should be always on your mind regardless of whether the team is ahead or behind. It matters.

Less than 5 minutes in the half – Each possession in a basketball game gains in importance as the clock winds down. Depending on how the situation is carried our, one team may attempt more 3-point shots, try to run the shot clock down, consistently foul to send a player to the line, etc.

Game Flow – It is easy to get caught up in how fast the game is going. Players will toss the ball down the court or shoot quick shots rebounded and run down the other way. The beauty of audio sportscasting is how in charge the broadcaster is. You control what is seen and what is not seen. If the play on the court is going back and forth, verbally slow it down and describe each play. Unless you have a really bad memory, you should be able to recall what happened and how, then get back into the flow.

Don't just follow the ball - Often, one of the teams will attempt to "slow" the game after a certain point in order to gain their rhythm. This is the perfect time for you to describe off-the-ball movement (**Example**: *"Ellis is sitting on the outside of the arch waiting for the ball, fighting off Fields as the Rangers go into a 3-2 zone"*). Notice that this had nothing to do with the ball. Instead, this gave the anticipation that the player named Ellis might be doing something, that Fields might be able to steal the ball or defend him properly, that the Rangers are now changing their defense the suit the next offensive attack. This is why you were instructed to call.

Taking care of the voice – Save your voice for the big plays. Don't just call everything like it is the seventh game of the NBA playoffs with ten seconds to go in a tie game. Your voice may sound flat or monotone, especially when you are calling each and every play. Don't worry about it, your voice and ability will grow naturally as you progress. Most coaches usually take about 200-300 games before they are even considered developed. You aren't going to be any different. By calling as many games as you can, by developing yourself each day, you will grow into a sportscaster. How far you go depends on how much you continue to learn each day.

Lubricating the voice – Your voice is your tool, your meal ticket. Consider it like an engine, if you don't lubricate the engine with oil, it will burn up. The same will happen to your voice if you don't continually attempt to drink plenty of fluids. The best type of fluid for sportscasters is good ole H20 (aka water). Drinking soda pop or coffee might seem fine, but consider how much salt and other chemicals are in those drinks. Plus, they likely will make you belch or dry out your voice quicker than water. Aside from those reasons, water is also readily available and usually free. You will also have to regulate how much water or fluids you intake during the game, mainly because there isn't a bathroom break until the game is over.

Off The Court Action – Talking about what is happening off of the court can be tricky. It can be a part of the atmosphere of the basketball game (example: Head Coach Antoni is upset with the call by the refs and kicking up a storm after that basket was taken away from his team). But it can also distract from the actual game itself (**Example:** *Head coach Antoni is hot right now. He's screaming up a storm at the ref. He just is letting the ref have it*). What exactly does that do for the listener? Is the game still going on? If the head coach is acting that way, is the ref reprimanding him? If so, what happened? If you call too much of the play by play off the court, you miss what is happening on the court. If the coach gets kicked out of the game, that is one thing. If the coach is just "jawing" at a ref and nothing is coming up it, all it creates is good theater. Unfortunately, theater is more visual than mental, therefore it distracts more than it helps your broadcast.

THE SPORTSCASTER'S NOTEBOOK

A Hot Mic Can Get You Fired – Be aware of your surroundings. Even if your microphone is off during a commercial break or time out, be aware that other microphones may be on. That can be the thing that gets you fired, if your voice goes out over the audio/video with something stupid coming out of your mouth. Are you a professional or are you a hobbyist? We do not live in a forgiving time, especially with social media. You have people who don't like you because you aren't their personal favorite announcer, or they are resentful that you've achieved a sportscasting career. Whatever the reason, if you give someone an excuse, they will use it, so don't be saying stupid things over a hot microphone because once it is out there, it cannot be taken back and you will likely lose your job (if you work at a station) or access to the team (even if you are an independent operator).

Reference Points – Audio broadcasts don't allow people to see anything, especially where something is. You have to verbally give the cue to develop the mental picture for the listener. Points as in how you see the call (did it happen to the left or right, did it happen on the top of the court or bottom?). These things matter in how you describe each play. (**Example:** "*Wayne shoots a 15 foot jumper off the right side of the box which rims off left into the hands of Burl who turns and fires a chest-pass down to Canton on the opposite end of the court*"). The amount of detail given here has dramatically increased the action in the mental picture that a person has of the play.

Working with a Board Operator – If you have the luxury of not being your own board operator, you will still need verbal cues in order to allow them to know when you are taking a break. (**Example:** *We will be back right after this, 50-49 Bearcats up by one with 12 secs to go. You're listening to Ceni Basketball on KWJY News Talk 1000*). This type of example will allow your board operator to know when to cue an advertisement for a sponsor. SEE references for the game commercial log for more information.

Errors or Flubs – Everything has errors in it. This book probably does somewhere to. Even when its been rewritten about 5 times, every document could have a comma misplacement or a sentence that doesn't form correctly. The difference between you and a major sportscaster is the fact that the major sportscaster has about 500-1000 games under their belt. They have made most of the errors you will make, mainly because it is part of the process. Until you can call a game in your sleep (i.e. 500 games), it is understandable that you will make errors along the way. A comedian says the same material about 1,000 times prior to going up on stage and repeating it, just to make it sound spontaneous. Think of what you are doing as a sportscaster, you only get that chance once with a spur of the moment decision on how to make that call.

Spur of the Moment Interruptions – Expect the unexpected, even off of the court. You may get some guy who knocks off your headset. He may have done it by accident or just because he's a jerk. The trick is to ignore the problem, regain your composure as quickly as possible, call the rest of the game until a timeout or break occurs, then get someone nearby (athletic director, staff member) to take care of the problem for you. Getting you out of your game face is probably that guy's goal, mainly because he is jealous you are in a business he wants to be in. Never let a person get your goat.

Women vs. Men Playing – When sportscasting a game of women or men playing, the ultimate difference for you will be the speed involved. For a women's broadcast, you should attempt to have worked previously with tapes of men's games, calling them as best as you can. Then switch to a women's tape. You'll notice right away how easier you think it is to sportscast a women's game and you will likely perform better, faster. If you are going to call men's sports, I would suggest using a game tape of a higher level than the level you are calling (i.e. NBA tape for an NCAA game). Speed will still be an issue, but you will be able to catch up a lot quicker by adapting to the quickest speed first, then slowing down, rather than vise versa.

THE SPORTSCASTER'S NOTEBOOK

Things to say during free throws – Instead of just rattling off numbers, describe how the player is making the free throw. You can also use some of the personal information about the player (**Example:** *"Gwen, a sociology major who was named student-athlete of the week back in December, crouches up with the first shot of this one-and-one free throw attempt which bounces off to the left of the rim, no good"*). Sometimes there is a long stretch of dead time in between a free throw, about 10-15 seconds where the floor is being mopped or a player is talking with her coach. You can use this opportunity to promote the next broadcast, give some upcoming schedule or team information.

Blue Language By Outside Forces – Sometimes a coach or a fan will curse up a storm on the sidelines or in the crowd, and your microphone will pick up all of it. There is nothing you can really do about this, and it happens to every sportscaster at least 20 times in their career. Either pot down the floor microphone, if you have on, or just attempt to cover your headset receiver with your hand when hearing this. However, if it is random or uncontrollable, just ignore it.

Eating During The Broadcast – Some sportscasters believe they can show up with a sandwich and eat it during the timeouts. This doesn't work and instead makes for a horrible audio broadcast. It also makes it more likely that the sportscaster will feel bloated or have to go to the bathroom. Don't fall into this trap; eat about 2 hours prior to game time. Your stomach and the listeners will thank you.

Fake Play-By-Play Southern Accents – They sound stupid, really. You may be able to fool some people with it, but really, you are making fun and offending an entire region of the country. And it sounds terrible.

Angry Coaches or Players – If a coach or player is angry after a tough loss, it is best not to bring them onto the program after the game unless they have some obligation to do so. If they do come on, remind them that they have to be a professional, that you are not there to make them look bad, and that you need them to be good content for the listener/viewer. The majority, even at the semi-pro or high school level, will get it right away and help you out. If you end up with a grumpy bear type coach who is always sullen after a loss, don't use them at all. It's not worth your time, or their time, to listen to a tirade that your viewership has to experience.

Show prep prior to the game – A good rule of thumb on show prepping is to start about 24 hours prior to tip-off. Look up every stat imaginable on the team that you are playing, speak with your team's coaching staff and get inside details. Understand as much as you can about the team, about its next opponent, and about the season thus far. I would attempt to schedule a consistent meeting with the coaching staff the day prior the the game (usually trying to schedule a day of game meeting with a coach doesn't work, for obvious reasons).

THE SPORTSCASTER'S NOTEBOOK

Things to do prior to tip-off:

1. Arrange your notes in a show prep binder. Section them off into different subjects:

a. Historical details on the team.

b. Stats of the season and last few games.

c. A roster sheet of home and away players, coaches.

d. Interesting details on individual players.

e. Stats of league standings and other teams.

2. Arrange your notes in a show prep binder. Section them off into different subjects:

a. Who, what, when, where, & how.

b. Give a pre and post intro, wrapped around an intro bed which allows you to flow into the sportscast.

Things to know prior to tip-off:

1. Memorize the names of all of your team's players and coaches. Know them by sight.

2. Find out how exactly who the players are, know as much on their playing and personal background as you can.

3. Find out the little things going on with the team (not gossip, but details) which will help your sportscast sound professional and well-done.

4. Find last year's record, stats.

5. Search through a lot of newspaper records, see if there are articles or photos.

6. Everything you do for the home team, now do for the away team. Try to give your listener the most in-depth broadcast in order to help enliven the mental picture for them.

7. Know as much as you can about the opponent that your team is facing, as well as the next opponent after that. You should know who the opponent has played.

8. You should know what happened in the last two games for the both the home team and the away team. Know all of the nuisances of the season for both teams. This will increase your sportscast.

Interviews – One of the most important aspects of interviews is how to properly do it. Yes, there is a right and wrong way here. Ask open ended questions, not yes or no questions. Mainly because if you ask a yes or no question, you get a yes or no question. One of the bad habits to break is the phrase "talk about..." which some reporters on-air attempt to ask. This seems less about asking a question than filling time. Most of the interviewees asked this question seem more annoyed by it than actually answer it correctly.

Good questions to ask:

1. What happened in the last ten seconds of the game that turned the tide for you down the stretch?

2. How are you dealing with the loss tonight?

3. What are you doing to improve this season?

4. I noticed you changed the lineup tonight, why?

Bad questions to ask:

1. Did you like the game?

2. Does it feel good to win the game like this?

3. Are you going to win next week?

THE SPORTSCASTER'S NOTEBOOK

Interview Parrots – When interviewing players who are in high school or college, you have to understand that they are still kids. Most of the time, they want to impress you and are willing to parrot back exactly what you say to them, because they really aren't thinking of the ramifications of what you are asking. Most are thinking about their last date, Ipod, or what they are going to eat after the game.

With this in mind, be careful what you ask a high school or college player, typically they are not used to the media attention and could say anything.

Don't get them in trouble for absolutely no reason (if they didn't commit a crime, don't treat it like an interrogation), and realize that if they find it fun to be interviewed, more of their fellow players will do the same, and you can count on their parents and family to listen to your broadcasts. A lot of what you can get a player to say can get them in trouble with their team, administrators, etc. Keep this in mind when considering what questions you are going to ask.

An Interview Parrott Question:

1. Do you hate player so-and-so when you face their team?
2. Your coach yells a lot during the game, doesn't he?
3. You were pretty much the only one who could score tonight, weren't you?

Chapter Seven

*Developing
Your
Color Analyst Skills*

Blowouts – It is unnecessary to tell your listeners that a blowout has happened, especially too early in the game. Why? Because you have an obligation to sponsors and the teams to attempt to "hold" those listeners for most if not all of the game. If you do say it's a blowout, it better be at the end of the game in order to gravitate the situation further in the listener's mind. Don't make fun of another team in a blowout, instead, attempt to be creative and talk about who the next opponent is, give some good examples of what the losing team did (if any), and what concerns the team needs to address. The last thing you want to say is: *"it's the first quarter and this game is over,"* mainly because your listeners will tune out and your sponsors will be upset with the result. This is Billy Packer Syndrome: The color analyst for CBS Sports' NCAA Tournament ended his 34-year career by being fired in 2008, after uttering "this game is over" during the 34-18 Kansas lead over North Carolina in the semi-final game. Granted, Kansas won the game, but still, it ticked off enough advertisers and network folks that the job Packer had been doing since 1975 was ended in 2008 with a whimper.

Amateur vs. Pro Rule – Being a player who is criticized by the on-air person sucks. Especially if you are an amateur (i.e. High school, college, rec league, lowest minor league). The fact is, a player at that level is trying their hardest, playing the game without seeking compensation, as is in many ways, learning, just like you are. There is a BIG difference between being an amateur and being a pro, one of them is the criticism you receive. Plus, at the lowest level, if you criticize some high school kid, their parent might listen. A few things that can happen to you if you offend a parent: Loss of sponsorship, loss of broadcasting right to the games (the PTA might pull the plug on you) and loss of life (parents are nuts anyway, why antagonize them?).

Knowledge – Attempting to "wing" a broadcast is a recipe for disaster, especially if you are serious about attempting to develop yourself as a sportscaster. Imagine if the players on the court did not practice, or slacked off practicing. How good would those players be in game action? Being "lucky" in a broadcast doesn't mean you are prepared. So start "show prepping."

Officiating – Referees are usually some of the best and worst of the sport. Mainly due to who you root for and what happens in the game. People are human. Therefore, you shouldn't attempt to ride the refs when they make bad calls. You can mention it, you can come back to it if the play really turned the tide in the victory, but don't keep focusing on it. Listeners want to hear about the action, not a running commentary on something that may or may not make the newspapers the next day. Besides that, you don't want to look like a homer, instead, try to look homespun.

Homer vs. Homespun – Some sportscasters attempt to really be in the thick of things and call everything as if the world is against their team. This is not professional and in fact, can backfire on the sportscaster. Saying things on the air like "*We got screwed by the refs*" or "*They aren't calling fouls on so-and-so*" is not classy. Remember that half of your audience might be the opponent's fans. They deserve to hear a good broadcast, even one which originates for the other team, rather than just a homer sportscast where everything can't be trusted. Being homespun means that you know the game, call the details of it accordingly, and happen to be interested more in the excitement of your team doing well rather than the other guy.

THE SPORTSCASTER'S NOTEBOOK

Know the game – This is one of the things that sounds easy, but takes a lot of work. Know each of the calls by the refs, why they are making those calls, what offenses and defenses are being made by the teams, and why substitutions are being made. Simply assuming makes you look like an amateur.

Calling out a player or coach on the air – While it may seem like you are doing *"what sports is all about"* but calling out a player or coach is stupid. First, the players are likely trying as hard as they can, and you may be offending someone by your comments (especially if they are student-athletes). Second, calling out a coach is stupid. It may get you punched or kicked out of the gym or off that school/team's broadcasts for good. Why? Because coaches know, may be friends with, or may just have a general respect for one another. A single listener can destroy your gig or at least make your life a living help by destroying your relationship with your own team.

Don't Say What Any Turkey Could – You need to give in-depth analysis, not retreated crap you've heard on ESPN or Fox Sports. This means being learning how each team runs a play, which plays they favor, the offensive and defensive schemes, and presenting a mental picture of each through verbal cues. Don't just say that a team is running an *"3-2 defense,"* describe it to the listener at least once per game, tell them exactly why a team would do that in order to defend the basket.

On Injuries - You are not a doctor. If you are a doctor, even then, you should not speculate on a possible injury during the sportscast in which the injury occurs. Too much is made of injuries anyway. If you have an injury confirmed by an athletic trainer, and it has been announced publicly, then use your discretion.

   If you are sportscasting a high school or college game, you might frighten a parent who is listening at home. This may cause you more grief than you want and may get people less likely to have you on the air.

If the injury looks serious, but isn't, you look like a fool. That basketball player who looked like he broke his leg and stumbled off to the locker room in the first half, but then ends up returning in the second half, scoring 40 points just made you look as if you don't know what you are talking about.

OTHER COLOR ANALYST NEEDS

Poker

A great way to engage your audience as a CA is to develop your CA skills without a PBP. I would highly recommend this as a way to expand your knowledge, while knowing how much you should and shouldn't say. Developing information that you use as a CA does not mean calling the action. Instead, it means telegraphing why the action happened or where it should be headed in order for an advantage to take place.

As the world has changed, so has its sporting tastes. Tribal casinos have used poker on video screens, along with sportscasting, as a way to engage their audience in the off-hours, when folks are not at the casino itself. This serves as an entertainment advertising, uploaded to YouTube, and keeps casual gamblers interested in the game itself. These types of sportscasts don't really require PBP as much as CA in order to thrive. It is a good exercise to utilize YouTube poker videos, turn off the sound, and describe what each advantage is and is not, in the role of a CA, for the viewer at home.

"Trent is watching the dealer lay down the river… and he didn't not get the card that he was looking for. Will he stay in on the bluff?"

"Jane holding a 85 percent after the three card flop, against Vance's 25 percent, as he has to hope for some luck as the dealer pulls out the next two cards."

It is also important to understand the sportscast is about the poker, but also about the verbal interaction that players have with each other. That's why a CA works more than an over-descriptive PBP. Because the players' smack talk matters as it engages the viewing audience. The CA has to be a balancing act between the two mediums of the sportscasting audio of analysis and the sportscasting broadcasting audio of the players bluffing each other.

Poker is something that you cannot wing. You need to know the game itself. Similar to blackjack and other gambling games. The CA needs to understand the various percentages, the reason behind each stake held or raised by the players at the table, and how to present that to the viewer at home. Tribal casinos have become big players in this type of sportscasting, and can pay larger sums to professional sportscasters to do it. The cameras are already embedded in the tables, but without sportscasters there to give insight, the presentation is lost and useless. Consider it a way to get into sportscasting, as well as get paid to do it long-term.

eSports

eSports has become a hot commodity for sportscasting. Twitch has provided numerous opportunities for sportscasters to join teams, providing play-by-play for groups of people who want to feel as if their talents are just as good as those players who use a live action ball on the court or field. Plus, eSports pays big money to sportscasters for the ability to have play-by-play called, and will also hire CA talent for the entire presentation. A lot of the Twitch and YouTube presentations are not on traditional television, but sportscasters can develop a large following through digital reach by doing these types of events.

eSports never really does PBP as much as recap of scores, interest and highlighting during the actual match. They are setting the stage of the players involved, as well as how each player has faired the tournament leading up to where they are now. eSports games tend to go fast, with the action in such a virtual form that it is not possible to constantly do a PBP set with a graphic character or different form spinning, moving almost beyond eyeball speed strength. When talking about the action, it is best to say mini-recaps of several action points within the last couple of minutes.

"Look at how Sarah took away John's power bar, three, now four times in a row with that spin kick somersault."

"John embracing a hide-a-go-seek tactic which is reducing Sarah's ability to counter."

It is also important to lay off talking during cut-scenes. These scenes are implanted into the game for a reason, and it distracts when sportscasters try to talk over them. Let the entire cut-scene play out as it would. The main PBP and CA interaction has less to do during the game action and more to do during the breaks in the action, where they will recap and present the audience with what happened and what is about to happen.

Chapter Eight

The Sports Talk Format

Format: Single Announcer

This is one of the most popular ways for sports talk radio to exist. Because the callers become the show, and the announcer presents the topic, then allows the callers to react. There is a 5-second delay system in case each caller says something "blue" over the airwaves, thus protecting the radio station from FCC regulations. The host starts each hour of the show by discussing about one primary topic and two secondary topics, for the first 13 minutes. This is a solo job without any callers. It is pure setup, trying to engage the listeners to either decide to call in, or get energized for the rest of the show. The setup asks questions, presenting them as if they can be solved within the hour.

THE SPORTSCASTER'S NOTEBOOK

Example: *"On today's show, we are going to be discussing last night's game. Everybody saw it. Especially the ending where the last second foul changed the score. What did you think about that? Should the coach have changed his defense to avoid that scenario? Usually these are games that the players step up in, and yet, the ending proved otherwise. Are we at a point where the players aren't listening to the coach? What does that say?"*

What this presentation does is allows those who have called in to "fill up the phone lines" during the commercial break prior to coming back to the single announcer, who then engages them during the rest of the three segments of the show.

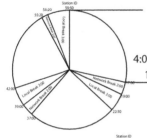

0:15 to 0:35 - INTRO INTO THE FIRST HOUR TOPICS
0:35 to 2:00 - TEASE LAST 42 - 55:20 SEGMENT
2:00 to 4:00 - TEASE 22:30 - 37:00 CALLER SEGMENT
4:00 to 16:00 - RANT ABOUT BIG TOPIC "LAST NIGHT'S GAME"
16:00 to 17:00 - TEASE PHONE LINES / CALLER SEGMENT

22:30 to 24:00 - RECAP THE FIRST SEGMENT RANT
24:00 to 26:00 - TEASE LAST 42 - 55:20 INTERVIEW
26:00 to 34:00 - FINAL SEGMENT TOPIC
34:00 to 36:00 - TEASE SECOND HOUR TOPIC
36:00 to 37:00 - TEASE FINAL SEGMENT TOPIC

42:00 to 45:00 - INTRO INTO THE FINAL SEGMENT OF HOUR
45:00 to 53:00 - FINAL SEGMENT LIVE INTERVIEW ETC
53:00 to 54:00 - SUM UP HOUR TOPICS QUICKLY
54:00 to 55:20 - TALK UP NEXT HOUR'S TOPICS

Format: Dual Announcer

This format tends to go away from the callers, instead relying on show prep and guests to fill the void of the entire hour. This is one of the more commonly used podcast formats as well. Two people talking over the topics in sports. Dual announcers have the ability to tease a lot more information and interest, keeping the audience "hooked" as the show progresses. While there are some potential callers during a radio broadcast, with a podcast format, this is nearly lot unless there are recorded audio messages. The format isn't about the caller carrying the show with their opinion against the reaction from the host, instead, its about staying mainly with the dual announcers as their opinions for the show are primary without any real secondary opinions causing conflict.

Format: Forum

This format stays away from callers entirely until it is determined that a "call-in" segment is being initiated. This call-in segment lasts usually for five or less total callers per hour, and allows the forum – made up experts in the sports field (or journalists who believe themselves to be experts in the field – the opportunity to provide insight as they serve as wisdom providers to the listening/viewing audience. This is not a bad overall format, but one that cannot be sustained daily for a five-day a week show.

42:00 to 45:00 - INTRO CALLER TOPICS
45:00 to 53:00 - LIVE CALLERS
53:00 to 54:00 - SUM UP HOUR OF CALLERS QUICKLY
54:00 to 55:20 - TALK UP NEXT HOUR'S TOPICS

0:15 to 02:00 - INTRO CALLER TOPICS
2:00 to 15:00 - LIVE CALLERS
16:00 to 17:00 - SUM UP CALLERS QUICKLY

22:30 to 24:00 - RECAP THE SEGMENT OF CALLERS
24:00 to 26:00 - PRESENT LIVE CALLER TOPICS
26:00 to 34:00 - LIVE CALLERS
34:00 to 36:00 - SUM UP CALLERS QUICKLY
36:00 to 37:00 - TALK UP NEXT HOUR'S TOPICS

Producing: Where It Starts

If you want to be working at a sports talk radio station, you may end up serving as a producer to someone else's show first. Prior to being the talent that carries a show, this is how you broke into the business. But that's all changed with livestreaming and podcasting. You have the ability to do both of those things – producer and host – through digital channels. At a radio station, however, there is a long line of people, namely men, who have been producing sports talk shows for years before they get a chance at the microphone. Doing both – the idea of working at a radio station and developing your own podcast or livestream where you act as the host, is not a bad thing. It hones your skills. It makes you better. Unfortunately, people wait around to allow their talent to be discovered. This doesn't help you get better, and in fact, it makes it more likely that you won't move from the producer job to the host job, because you will be green despite the years of the experience working as a producer on the show.

The great thing about being a producer is that it allows you to "cut your teeth" learning how to manufacture guests for the host, develop show prep content, blend topics, record or highlight plays or interview clips from other broadcasts, and screen callers to ensure that there is quality control for the show. A producer is the invisible hand that guides the show forward, while the host takes a lot of the credit and gets it. Producing is a tough, thankless, what-have-you-done-for-me-lately job that everyone requires for their show to go smooth, but few people outside of other producers, actually understands.

Producing: Guest Prospecting

The closest thing to guest prospecting is if you decided to do telemarketing inquiries in high school. Doesn't matter if it was over the phone or by instant messenger or by e-mail, it all relates. Not only do you have to sell the guest on the fact that they should be on your show, you have to arrange a time in which they need to either call back into the radio station line or a time in which you can call them on their phone. And you have to pray that their cell phone connection won't die halfway through the interview because their reception is horrid. This circus also needs to be coupled with the fact that the talent needs to be ready for the guest entirely. Several factors may be at play that makes coordination a challenge; that the previous guest on the show or callers leading up to the next guest haven't gone over the segmented time on the radio's hour clock. You also have to be sure that the guest will actually remember to be ready for the call. Guest prospecting can be fun, as long as you do not get star struck if you get that guy to go on the air with your host who struck out 10 batters last night or just won the league MVP.

There are also four rules to follow when performing guest prospecting:

Rule 1: Be professional and courteous. Tell them what the topic of the show is, how they fit into it, and make them aware of how much time they have to cover it with the guest. Do not attempt to ambush them or it will get around the sportscasting community that the show is not a good one, and you will start to see guests decline to come on entirely.

Rule 2: Find a time that works for both you and the guest. If you have a morning show, and need the interview to be on the air at 6:30 a.m. Pacific Coast Time (PST), you either have to record the guest in the afternoon, or try to lock in guests who are located on the East Coast, so that the time difference makes it more manageable. Understand that you are not the only show producer demanding of their time.

Rule 3: Make sure that you have more than enough show prep on the guest ready for the host to use. Some host talent end up doing a lot of show prep themselves, but others tend to be small town jerks who show up at the radio station, waiting for the producer to do all of the actual leg work. The worst radio interview ever is one to where the talent knows nothing about the guest, hasn't performed or be provided with research, and makes assertions that flatline the interview entirely, creating awkwardness and dead air. Your job as a producer is to ensure that the bad interviews do not happen. Even if you don't like the host, or think that he is ill-equipped for the hosting position, it is your job to make him sound great.

Rule 4: If something happens, be flexible. Have a backup plan for additional show prep or another segment in order to make up for the fact that the guest could not make the show, thus cancelling that hour's segment. Don't allow the host to criticizing the guest on the air for not coming on – there may have been a family emergency or other scheduling conflict unknown that demanded the guest's attention. It does not speak well of the host or the producer if criticism over a cancellation occurs, especially when the reasoning for the cancellation is unknown.

Producing: Highlight Clips

The best highlight clips have relevance back to the overall story segment, lasting less than 2 minutes in overall length. Simply finding every homerun call to place into a highlight clip does nothing of the listener/viewer to understand and digest the content accordingly. You have to continually think about what makes every highlight interesting in that clip. The listener/viewer needs to care. Imagine if there were a highlight clip full of play-by-play every time a batter walks, or did something mundane. The power of the homerun is its limited availability to see – not every batter hits a homerun, and not every game has homeruns, so it makes it elusive and interesting. When you place a ton of homeruns together, in a continuous cycle, with zero context toward the game story, you lose the magic. Make your highlight clips interesting. Make them real. Mix the entire thing up. Every game has more than one story, one piece of drama, going on, regardless of whether its basketball, baseball, football or even eSports. Your job is to discover the actual reason that the highlight clip is interesting and worth using.

Producing: Interview Clips

An entire press conference is great for YouTube, Facebook or website listeners who want to want to watch the entire three hour show. But in reality, the majority of viewers want something in 30 seconds or less. That means that the long reporter questions or interviewee lame jokes need to be saved for unedited content.

Instead of simply being a record and broadcast producer, you need to cut the interview down to the heart of the story. What happened that makes this interview interesting? Specifically, what answers did the interviewee give which will make the listener/viewer turn up the volume in their car, their earbuds or on their smart TV to hear it and continuing digesting the content? If an interview is boring to you as the producer, is to by far 10-times more boring to your listeners who are trying to digest it. Coach press conferences are only interesting if you cut up the content into highlights, focusing on the most important answers regarding the team. Put these out into several 30 second-to-1 minute video segments on Facebook, scheduled at different times. The comments, shares and likes will go through the roof as you start to engage an audience that only has this small amount of time for the team in general.

Producing: Segment Creation

The talent has a lot to say in the daily and weekly meetings about segment creation on radio and podcasting. Hosts typically focus on larger issues for each show rather than the specific quarter hours. Segment creation, every quarter hour of a 4-to-5 hour show, is where the producer either shines or sinks. Segment creation means taking a mixed salad approach to the show itself. Simply allowing the talent to "throw open" the phone lines does nothing for the show, exposing the show to the danger of having less people call, and providing a less interesting program in general to listen to.

SEGMENT CREATION: 12 p.m. to 1 p.m.
Interview: Jack Stone – Times Reporter; Interview Ryan O'Landry – Western Athletic Director
Caller Phone Lines: 12:35 p.m.
Phone: 555-555-5555
Phone Topic: Braves Football Loss To Cal last weekend.
Phone Topic: Stevens Dropped Catch At M's Game, 12th Straight Loss
Highlight Clips: 12:42 p.m., 12:55 p.m. Stevens Interview (taped)

Producing: Blended Topics

Part of producing a great show is understanding that you have to be diversified. That means consistently talking about one topic, all of the time, whether it be on a radio sports talk show or a podcast, will garner you less and less of an audience. Remember that you have soccer fans, American football, basketball, baseball, hockey and mixed martial arts (MMA) fans. And they want to listen to a variety of things. Even if they love, specifically, their sport, they also have other interests. And you have a mixed salad of an audience to cater to. Talking five hours of golf coverage every day on the radio for a sports talk station, up against a local baseball or basketball team that is top of the standings, is likely to get you a reprimand from the program director rather than a raise. Conversely, podcast sports talk decisions tend to fizzle out after a few episodes, mainly because they rely so heavily on one subject, over and over again, that it becomes repetitious and disinteresting, even to that hardcore listenership.

The great sports talk shows know how to blend the topics of golf and football and baseball and hockey into a multi-use program. The more you stick primarily to one topic, the less that audience will stick around after a certain period of time. Every sport has some value, but is also fighting that sport's niche, beyond the headlines, providing insight to your listenership/viewership, which makes the difference maker on whether they continue to listen later on. Especially in the podcast world where one unsubscribe click can eliminate you from their listening choices forever.

Your job in a sports talk format is to target a piece of your audience (say MMA) for a quarter hour, then switch over to another topic of another sport, that maybe your audience isn't as interested in but still, you keep them because while they may not entirely care about the new topic, they know in less than 15 minutes, you will be talking about football or another sports topic that they do talk about. Local sports talk stations should focus on a quarter system of two-fourths local, two-fourths national in terms of topic coverage. It means that you are hitting every aspect of the day entirely, keeping interest of the audience so that they don't unsubscribe or tune out of what you are talking about.

Producing: Feeding Callers To Host

Part of the sports talk radio's dirty little screen is how they call screen. This is where producers earn their money by prepping their callers with more topic ammo than the general public ever realizes. Some of the producers that have horrible callers tend to be lazy at call screening. They simply answer the phone, ask you what topic you want to talk about, and boom, put you in line to talk to the host. Other producers answer the phone, talk to you for 5-10 minutes about whatever you are saying, rephrase it back to you in a more concise manner, then hone your call until it is something that the Sports Talk Topic Tree can used. The host wants this type of high-energy, concise caller to focus the listenership into leaning in for the whole segment.

THE SPORTSCASTER'S NOTEBOOK

TOPIC TREE SEGMENTS

INTRO – LEAD
SUBJECT #2
SUBJECT #1
SUBJECT #1

Example of Topic Tree

- **STEROIDS IN BASEBALL**

- **IS ROGER MARIS STILL THE HOMERUN KING?**

- **THROW OUT THE STATS?**

- **SHOULD MARK MCGWIRE BE IN THE HALL OF FAME?**

This topic tree example shows how one basic topic can spawn into several different thoughts on the same subject. The purpose is to help a host when the topic gets hot so that they can continue to keep the conversation going into different directions, but keep the listenership focused. The talent can really discuss everything on-air, but use the topic tree, along with the line of callers, to really pepper the conversation forward. Remember, on-air radio broadcasting is still expensive and valuable real estate. The callers also know this, because the producer has prepped them ahead of time, told them that they only get a couple of minutes at most to make their point to the host, and thus, the magic happens in a rapid fire conversation where everyone is ready to go.

Some callers don't get it. They aren't there to be focused. They are all over the place. Sometimes you have to work out the bugs of a caller's message in order to get that gem from them positioned on the air when they talk to the host. Some thoughts on call screening include telling them to be energetic, concise in a blunt enough manner.

EXAMPLE:

Producer: Station KWIW Sports Talk?

Caller: Hi, This is Jerold. I want to talk to the announcer on the air.

Producer: What's your subject?

Caller: I want to talk about the basketball team's record.

Producer: What's wrong with their record?

Caller: They are 10-23!

Producer: Yeah, but what would you do to change the team around?

Caller: Fire the coach and GM for starters.

Producer: So, you really want to talk about firing the coach and GM?

Caller: Well, yeah, I mean, we do not even run good plays, I think we aren't practicing enough on the defensive end of the court.

Producer: You mean how we lost our last five ball games by 20 points or more?

Caller: Yeah.

Producer: Okay, repeat what you want to say to me. All of it. Hit me with it.

Caller: We need to fire the coach and GM. We're 10-23 and we don't even run good plays because we aren't practicing enough on the defensive end of the court. We've lost our last five games by 20 points or more. Something's got to give.

Producer: That sounds great. Make sure you say it like that so our listeners get everything. You gotta lot of knowledge, man. You'll be next up after the great so be ready.

Notice that the producer focused the caller's subject, tailoring it to what needed to be said. First, the caller was complaining generically. The producer questioned exactly what was wrong, which was the team's record. Then the producer asked more about what the caller would do, learning that the caller's solution is to fire the coach and GM.

Instead of being satisfied, the producer continued to focus the caller until it came out that the caller really wanted to talk about the team's lack of defense and practice.

Then producer used all of that information, through active listening, and fed the caller a statistic to make the caller's argument more effective, allowing it to have merit to the listening audience. The producer then reminded the caller that what they were saying would be heard by the listening audience. Yes, the producer fed the caller a summed up statement for the caller to use on the air to the host. Yes, the caller's argument had to be mashed together into a coherent manner. But, so what? The sports talk format is entertainment. Absolute, pure entertainment. Callers who are uninteresting are not entertaining. They are boring. Which means no one wants to listen to them at all.

Producing: Handling The Talent

Small market radio or television talent is the worst to deal with if you are the producer of their show. Mainly because they are typically frustrated people who spend their entire life consumed with anger that they are not an emerging big time talent working in a large market. They are also people who cannot help but be consumed with every little detail of mismanagement. They also enter the building late, do not even attempt to do show prep, road block innovative ideas to improve the show because those ideas are not their own, and they "wing it" whenever they choose to, which is often.

The best way to handle talent is to do the best job that you can for them, then move onto another gig. Leave that sullen person behind.

Another word for talent is underachiever, specifically because talent after a while has to be crafted into a skill set. When you are talented with over a decade of experience in the field, its because you no longer are growing, but instead, still show a bit of differential between you and everyone else. Do not repeat their mistakes yourself. The reason some people remain or exist in a small market situation is because of their crappy attitude, their inability to get along with others, and their ineffective professional development of their craft. If your goal is to be in a big market as an entertaining sports talk host, you need to be patient, avoid a small market mentality, and work hard at becoming better at your craft.

Producing: Daily/Weekly Show Meetings

These meetings are designed to go over the basic topics of the show. To hit all of the points, in terms of what guests are schedule, what information is slated to be ready. Some talent will be more interested than others in attending these meetings and learning from them. The more prepared everyone is, the more interesting the show. A daily meeting lasts no more than 10-15 minutes, and is held an hour prior to the show's broadcast. This briefing is to go over those guests scheduled, what topics really matter and to hand whatever show prep the talent needs to use on-air, especially last night's game stats, etc. The weekly meetings are held on a Monday, about two hours prior to the show, lasting no more than 30-45 minutes, allowing both the talent and the producer to talk through any coordination issues that they felt came up during the show from the week prior, and figuring out ways to correct them for the upcoming week. Meetings are the only way to fully prepare a sports talk show and consistently improve the program's quality.

Producing: Live Remotes

Some of the worst sports talk radio is performed via live remotes.

These remotes are done from a location in-stadium, or at a sponsor's business such as a bar, but are a necessary evil toward the radio station making money. It's the bottom line part of the business. Podcasts have also made this attempt at working live, on stage, with an audience. The presentation is less than stellar. There are reasons that audio sportscasting or sports talk has a bit of separation between it and the audience. You may wonder why you can hear the action of the game along with PBP, those are separate microphones hooked up – one is in the quiet booth with the PBP and the other microphone is aimed at the field, where it picks up the noise of the crowd. There has to be some separation to build presentation.

When live remotes occur, you often hear the clanking of dishes as the crowd decides to watch and eat, or talk amongst themselves while the program is going on. A producer will sometimes have to work with a board op back in the studio who will act as a call screener, and who will also play sponsor ads during the breaks. The producer focuses on the people at the remote, the live audience, who can be placed on the show via a stand-up microphone, aimed at the talent on stage. The producer also acts as a gopher for the talent to get drinks, etc. Live remotes only pay off in sponsorship dollars, never in actual presentation. There are too many variables which make it more difficult and unreasonable for the audience at home to want to watch/listen in general.

Producing: Cell vs. Landline

Cell phone reception is a horrible audio tool for audio/video streaming. They typically have less bars in less areas than advertised.. Cell phone callers also sound as if they are on a permanent speaker phone. Whenever possible, especially with guests, get them to call in on a landline for interviews or when talking open phone line calls. Now there are some options today that weren't available today when this book was written in 2008. Both Skype and Zoom have figured out ways, if the caller attaches their smart phone to a WiFi signal, to allow the smart phone to sound as if they are using an in-studio microphone. The sound quality has improved greatly along with the advent of technology. Cellular connections alone sound like crap over radio or other audio streams, especially when the call is starting to drop and begins to sound garbled on-air.

Talent: Controversial Is Not Conversational

You can be the biggest talk of the town for about a month, maybe a bit more than a month, by offending everyone over the air. You can have your own podcast and rage on everyone, calling them stupid, and getting a lot of trollish traffic. It's not difficult to call out everyone else in the sports community. You can lead the bandwagon to get the coach fired, or a player benched. You can say mean, nasty things, making everyone listen to you to hear what you will say next.

And then, in a month or two, you can be out of a job. Why? Because sports talk needs listeners, but it also needs guests. The audience also does not respect out-of-control people for very long, especially when you start lighting up the town's favorite player or coach. People will put up with it for a while, but much like a Facebook post, the interest in it subsides. People move on. And if the only thing you have to add is negative, people soon tune you out.

Being controversial will not sell for long. It's a cheap Carnie trick. It's hack. And it will get you kicked out of your job once people no longer pay attention to you. Once you are mean, it's hard to return to nice.

Talent: Callers

Insulting the callers to your sports talk show is a great way to get yourself out of the sports talk field. Callers are listeners. The more listeners who are angry, or tune you out, the less audience you end up keeping for your show tomorrow and the next day.

THE SPORTSCASTER'S NOTEBOOK

A great example of this is the late Mike Responts (1960 – 2012), known in Boise as "The Sports Pig." His sports talk show was carried back in the 1990s overnights throughout the nation. He would end most calls by saying "*You're A Loser, and Your Team's A Joke.*"

His national show ended abruptly, and he died in obscurity in Boise, Idaho, off-the-air, because no sponsor wanted to pay to listen to that type of noise. It seems funny to hear at first, but when you are a caller at the receiving end, it seems less funny. And over time, few people call in, because they don't want to be the victim. Which kills the show overall because it is less entertaining, and less relevant.

There is a blog post up to him by a colleague, John Rabe, which seems to be about the only memory left of Mike Responts online at all – no sportscasting Hall of Fame induction. No mp3s of his shows are listed anywhere to hear his voice. It didn't matter how talented or skilled that the person was while discussing sports. Once the audience leaves, there's no reason to keep someone like that on the air.

Talent should always try to respect the caller's opinion, hear them out, and argue with each caller effectively. There is a difference between argue and insult. Just because you have a forum to speak the loudest – sports talk – does not mean that you have the only true opinion. Speak in sports that refer back to the disagreement with the caller, but make sure that the caller understands that you respect their point of view as well. Remember, you and the caller have adjoined in this conversation to be entertaining to the listener/viewer at home. Insulting those who are helping build your show does nothing to keep it entertaining at all.

Example:

Talent: Steve, welcome to Sports Radio 820.

Steve: Hi, Bill, I think we should fire the coach because we are 10-23 this season.

Talent: Well, it's the mid-point of the season, Steve.

Steve: But that doesn't make it right to see the bad performance out there. We've lost our last five games by 20 points or more. Something has to change.

Talent: Look, Steve, I'm not defending the coach when I say this, but I do think that since we won the division last year, we should give him a bit more of a chance. Don't you? Thanks for the call though.

Notice that the Talent allowed Steve to make his point without insulting Steve for his opinion. He didn't refer to Steve as a moron, or an idiot, for wanting the coach fired. Instead, the Talent pointed out what he felt were good reasons to keep the coach, thus keeping the argument civil and interesting. He also thanks the caller for calling in, thus retaining the caller as a listener. Neither side went away from the subject feeling as if they were ignored or cut off or not treated with equity in the conversation. No one felt insulted. There is a higher likelihood that it also made two or three of the listeners feel encouraged to call up, argument their opinions even if they are unpopular against those of the host, and not feel as if they are going to get bashed for expressing what they have to say.

Talent: Intro Segments

As shown on the format wheels prior, each hour allows the Talent to "reset" the conversation entirely. Podcast episodes perform the same task, doing a "reset" at the start of each episode. This allows the talent to fully expand what is going to be discussed throughout the entire hour in an intro segment. The segment starts out as a rant, focusing on one specific subject, usually a game or an issue that is facing a team or a specific sport, then it teases listeners with what is coming up for the rest of that hour, or podcast episode. This segment is 8-12 minutes on the radio hour clock, but perhaps only two minutes in a podcast episode.

THE SPORTSCASTER'S NOTEBOOK

Example:

Talent: *"The Braves lost their twenty-third game last night, yet something we have come to now expect from the clowns on the bay occurred. I watched the broadcast in horror as YET another game dropped from a team that won the division last season. This is frightening. This is NOT Braves basketball. Last time I checked, the guy coaching the team did not subscribe to this type of bad basketball either. What happened? We'll discuss with Jack Stone of The Times, who covers the Braves beat daily, and was there at the Forum last night, watching the whole thing go down. Also in this hour, Expect Kristen Jones to stop by with a report on the NASCAR season, plus your phone calls…"*

Talent: Guests

Every guest has something that they are selling. This is a new reality. No one is coming on just to come on the show. It may be a new season of the sport, inviting readers to pick up the latest newspaper/ blog to check out a sports column or an organization that they are a spokesman for. It could be books that they are trying to sell as well. Remember that with your guests, it is best to ask a question and be quiet.

I recommend muting your microphone after you ask the open-ended question, then letting them fill the void and talk. The listeners want you to ask the questions on subjects that they are interested in learning the answers about, but they want to hear the guest, not the host, answer those questions. This is a circus dance of epic proportions. Otherwise the show is just about the host and nothing else. There is no need for the guest to come on at all if they cannot finish a sentence, a statement or a thought because the host becomes interruptive.

The questions have to be asked: Why is the guest on the show? Why did the producer book the guest? Why did the host decide that the guest was relevant enough to join the show?

The host also needs to create a short recap of why the guest is on. Who the guest is and what importance they will bring to the show, as well as the listeners. It also shows that the talent has some clue as to who the guest is, and their relevance to the show.

Podcasting / Sports Talk - The world of sports talk has changed with audio/video livestreaming and podcasting. This allows you to be anywhere, give out your opinion, and doesn't require a television/radio station to do it. Sports talk is a key way to engage people in a set format. It's been around since the 1980s, shot through traditional radio as the next big thing, and now has a home on nearly every market, including digital audio/video such as podcasting and YouTube/Facebook. The sports talk format has seen its ups and downs, yet survived to some extent by virtue of its non-copyright ability to broadcast. Two people talking on a microphone is not something that someone else, aside from the two people, own, therefore it is more viable than the music rights format, which someone else owns, and you decide to play the music to. This chapter should help you attempt to navigate the format successfully. It is written more as as its own primer of advice, since, aside from the topic tree, there are no real extensive exercises to perform.

The goal of any sports talk show is to get listeners to continue to listen through each quarter break (15, 30, 44, top of the hour). This is how a radio station divides up its ratings, from the highest levels down to the lowest levels, of the industry. It is also how stations sell commercial advertising, so hitting that target audience, on radio, has been important since the quarter break system is crucial to the survival of any radio station.

That has changed with podcasting. You can run a podcast for 15 minutes or 15 hours. All you have to do is continue to be interesting. You have to know the entire subject, be willing to break it down, and use your SM profiles to alert fans when the latest podcast episode is out. I've personally used the podcast service Libsyn for several years, since I launched my own sports interview podcast, Tao of Sports, in 2012. From 2012 to 2018, I interviewed over 870 sports industry professionals, had a listenership of 15,000 consistent monthly downloads, and had 75 paid subscribers at $5 a month through a custom app. All of these things are possible as you initiate your sportscasting career.

But it matters that you are providing a consistent, listenable product that people want to hear. An example of a bad topic for sports talk listeners is a show about the latest bill going through Congress. Unless that bill is directly involved in sports (stadium construction, beer sales, limiting high school athlete eligibility, etc). While some of that talk may be permitted, assume that more of the sports talk format that an announcer thrives in is actual sports talk, not less. And the more than a sports talk announcer talks about non-sports related topics, the less likely that the listening audience will stay with them. While sports talk listeners are typically some of the most loyal, segmented audiences out there, they will tune out if they are not constantly being catered to. **SO TALK SPORTS.**

Podcasting is a more interesting medium that live radio when it comes to the sports talk format. The host has no way of accepting callers, thus must may several initiatives toward gaining the interest of the listener. They may be alone, or with a single guest, and be required to talk the audience into continuing its interest while the podcast is being played during a car ride, or in certain segments during a commute, several hours or days or months or years after that podcast was recorded. Sometimes, the content will not be "evergreen" and be dated, but still, the host has to ensure that people may want to listen to it. A podcast library is a valuable tool for sportscasters, and it continues to gain more listeners over time.

Sports talk on the radio has its different type of shine. Namely, that it can accept live callers who ask the host questions and otherwise engage with the show. It is important to remember that callers typically make up less than two percent of the listening audience in general. Most listeners are casual fans, seeking light entertainment away from the worries of the day, concerning themselves with something trivial which will not mean a life or death result. That is why talking about serious subjects is not advised (unless a local or national tragedy just occurred such as 9/11 or BLM boycotts at the NBA playoffs).

Chapter Nine

Hosting Team Watch Parties

When people think of sportscasters, they frame the position as one that is at the game or in the radio studio. They forget about the secondary sportscasters who are handling remote broadcasts that may not be aired to the general public, instead focusing on a specialized crowd. For example, a crowd that is in a restaurant. These are in some ways more exciting, with a limited audience, because of the engagement factor set forth between the sportscaster and those sitting in the seats. Sports watch parties are a thing. They are a big factor in driving fan excitement for upcoming games on the road, and they create an opportunity for those attempting to break into the business, or be a part of a team that already has a play-by-play announcer and color analyst set for their games. This is not a position or opportunity to look past.

There are also several dynamics to hosting a watch party for a team. Whether it be football, basketball or baseball, fans are giving up their time to go, pay money to eat a meal and/or drink a beer, and watch with a crowd. The least you can do as a sportscaster is make the experience as entertaining as possible. Doing this requires a venue, typically a restaurant or a casino eatery area, where there is a PA system (either portable or in-house) available so that the sportscaster can take charge of the event. That makes it possible for the crowd to not only watch the game, but play along with the in-house entertainment that they cannot receive if they sat at home on their couch. Watch parties are a way to defeat the issue of a disengaged audience sitting in front of their plasma TV at home because of the energy that the sportscaster on the microphone brings to the event itself. People want to have a focused, exciting time together with other like-minded fans with the excitement that comes out of being there at the venue. It is your job as a sportscaster to bring the heat, so to speak.

As the sportscaster, you are the head cheerleader for the event.

That means in the five minutes prior to the game on the big screen or several screens, you are up in front of everyone. You are drawing their attention, welcoming them to the experience that they are about to have. This is where you run the show with confidence. One thing that may look odd, but is necessary, is the ability to "eat the mic", which means to **rest the mic against your chin when you speak**. This may look odd but it will carry your voice in the mic system because there is nothing between you and the microphone diaphragm. Your voice needs to be constant, consistent, and ready to push out information amid every other sound in the venue. There could be televisions blaring or people talking, and this is a great way to command attention, because you are the biggest, booming voice in the room.

When you present the night's watch party, you should have rehearsed a lot of the standard information. Do not bring up a stack of cards and read off them. Remember, you need to be prepared. The less prepared you are, the audience will become more disinterested. You are there to walk the crowd through the entire ceremonies of the game. That means having set games already in mind that people can play throughout each quarter, period or inning. You should be hyping up those activities, with the set notion of giving out free merchandise, tickets, or other items of interest that keep everyone engaged. And this means more than simple giveaways. You need these activities to involve folks, to keep them throughout the game, even if there are uninteresting aspects such as their team getting blown out on the road.

Let's start with a football watch party, which is literally the easiest because it is built into a pattern of activities:

The **first quarter** should be something simple like bingo. Where you hand out bingo cards, let everyone play, and see what happens. These come despite or because of any score, and the prizes are small. Maybe work with the venue itself to hand out free beers if folks win at bingo. The great thing about bingo is that it allows for multiple winners, so everyone is on-board during the first quarter to be a part of the action. During this time, you want to hype up the halftime activities, which will be an eating or drinking contest. You want this to be something to where folks have to use their cell phones or fill out a paper entry form, something that engages them beyond the bingo card. You also need to have folks using their social media, taking photographs with hashtags for your event, with the ability to create photos of the night contests for the third quarter. This creates more activity with your crowds later on.

The **second quarter** should be something that is more sports trivia driven. This allows people who are sports nuts toward the team to show their ability to name different athletes or events that have occurred. The prizes need to be a bit bigger for this one, something tangible. With this, continue to hype up the halftime show, where you need to select three or four contestants. Everything needs to be setup with the venue, along with tables up front so everyone can watch the halftime. Once the trivia has hit its stride, with likely teams that will be playing, it is important to bring the crowd back to reality. Remember as the game is being played, there are plenty of giveaway activities with teams scoring or interceptions or penalties. But you are, at the end of the day, trying to invest these folks back into the show itself beyond the game on the screen.

Halftime needs to be an eating or drinking contest. This is where you have 22 ounce beers, a stack of hot dogs, or extra spicy chicken wings. There needs to be a real tangible prize, along with some specialized t-shirts, in order to make the activity worthwhile. Set up to eight people doing this. IF there are more than four people, then you need to have two rounds plus a final round – four people in each round, then the top two out of both rounds make up the final four. Essentially, this is more about bang for your buck entertainment. Every time that folks eat or drink more, the rest of the crowd gets into it. If you have the ability to have access to the big screen, you should have it where the rest of the crowd is placing bets, with 50 percent of the funds going to a local charity, and a betting line with someone actually placing bets. Doing this at a casino venue is one of the easier ones because it allows you to evade gambling laws. This is all about festive abuse, the type where everyone is in on the joke. Throughout the first half, there needs to be some analysis going on about each contestant, what their strengths and weaknesses are about eating, drinking, etc.

This should help people when they are making their bets and allows the line to move accordingly.

The **third quarter** is where it gets interesting. This is where the sportscaster needs to engage in the team fight song, but have audience members do it via an American Idol-type event with the crowd judging them. This way, it is a constant activity that reinforces the fear of missing out (FOMO) aspect and prevents people from leaving, even if the game on the screen sucks. Keep in mind that even with good football teams, there is a likelihood that the team may struggle that night. You have to be the other side of the entertainment coin. As a sportscaster, you need to have this audience leave the venue swearing that they will be returning for the following away game watch party because of how much fun it is. You should switch up the other songs, and perhaps do a few that have nothing to do with the game itself, simply to mess with the folks who are coming up. Remember, this is as much about entertaining comedy as it is the seriousness of the sport itself that they are watching.

The **fourth quarter** is where you hype up the next game. Where the action on the screen intensifies. You should also set interviews with former players or other team celebrities who you know are coming to the watch parties. Get them on the mic, get questions from the audience, and then ask them. Also, you should put up on the big screen those watch party photographs that are posted on social media with your hashtag and select winners of the party through that mechanism. Activity and engagement matter. This is a set war of how to have more fun than the experience at another event not run by your team. As a sportscaster, this is also a great audition for your own skills, as it ensures that anyone watching knows what you do to bring the show even when it's not calling the game on the court or field.

Keep in mind that the watch party is a mechanism for overall fan engagement at a time when the only way to otherwise access the game is on television. This works not only for road games, but for when the team is in a sold-out situation. One of the more mystifying things about sold-out home games is that the home team often does not provide these types of activities. They simply sell all their tickets, then abandon fans at the time when folks are the most interested. A watch party is something that you cannot get while sitting on the couch or dealing with a media rights territorial blackout situation.

Watch parties have always been specialty branded events for restaurant or casino venue activation. Those are the ones who are sponsoring the events and who should have a direct satellite feed capability to access those games even if they are blacked out. These should not be left to set up the night of the show or even within the week. These are set up months in advance. Remember, this is about keeping your fans engaged throughout the year, but also, when the team is on a back-to-back road trip where they are in a literal dead zone. Especially if the games are not carried on a regional sports network. And when territorial blackouts occur, these issues need to be hammered out by the team itself, especially if the team has already sold all their tickets. This is where the team needs to step it up, because once the team loses and the folks who have previously purchased season tickets have stopped doing so, it is incumbent to get those who have attended the watch parties to buy season tickets. This is their opportunity to do so. But only if the watch parties have conveyed the excitement of the team's games and brought the show. Keep in mind, if you are doing watch parties for smaller teams or collegiate teams, then it is imperative to also look at livestream functionality with the restaurant or venue IT long before the season starts. This also makes the watch party exclusive, meaning more fans will show up to the watch party because they cannot get it anywhere else. Exclusivity matters.

That is why breaking down each quarter, with set activities, changes the tone of the watch party. The event has to be special. Something to where if they leave after the second quarter, they are missing the fun at halftime or during the remaining two quarters. These high engagement opportunities also create that F.O.M.O. (fear of missing out) on social media. Not only through your posts, but those of the watch party attendees who are hashtagging the event with their own posts. This gets noticed by the fans who didn't attend the watch party but now want to know how to attend future watch parties themselves. And make certain that everyone knows that reservations for the upcoming watch parties are being taken now. Getting some fans shut out, because they waited until the last minute to make a reservation, sets another tone of getting everyone excited early and often and will ensure that they show up to be a part of the next event.

This is where the team's marketing, merchandise, and ticket staff need to be involved with the watch party. They need to have buy-in that this is a great opportunity show up with a portable team store at the restaurant or casino venue, ready to sell. Same with tickets. This should be treated as a regular game opportunity because revenue generation not only matters, but it ties back to folks wanting to listen, view or digest the broadcast and game later on. Consider that every fan you make will end up listening to the sportscast when they drive home away from that game at the arena or field. They will also have an affinity toward you as the sportscaster, and will be a driving force to allow you to get better overall.

Too often, broadcasters attempt to "appear above it all" when it comes to how the sausage (i.e. revenue / money) is made for a team. Broadcasters tend to view themselves as enough, when they are only a part of the show. It is nothing without the crowds and fans in the stands. Want to have a quick comparison? All major sports attempted to have games without fans during the 2020 COVID-19 restrictions. The NBA did this with the "bubble" in Orlando. It was terrible. Fans are one of the biggest ways that excitement occurs for a game. When you don't have excitement, the margin of victory doesn't matter. No fans equal a dead, empty void. Even a sportscaster doesn't do well in an arena or stadium without a crowd. Sure, the L.A. Lakers won the 2020 NBA title, but it wasn't the same without the electric crowd being energized with each shot, whether for or against the team. Fans matter. And as a sportscaster, especially when it comes to a watch party, you are there to get fans to want to buy tickets and merchandise and be a part of the overall arena or ballpark experience.

No broadcaster can be above generating new fans for the team. New fans equal new listeners. And it comes in all forms. This includes handling watch parties where you are the sportscaster in the restaurant, but someone else is the sportscaster on the television for the home team. You never know the opportunities that may exist in the future. Teams switch out lazy broadcasters all of the time, and if you bring an entertaining show to the restaurant or venue, that can translate toward an opportunity to do play-by-play for the team or another team somewhere else. You may be a broadcast or communications assistant, not the lead broadcaster, but that can change with opportunities. It comes down to taking each opportunity seriously. Watch parties are a successful blind spot for a lot of broadcasters who do not see the opportunities the same as you or I might. They might think that it is not enough to do in-restaurant experiences on the microphone, but everything is what you make of it. If you bring presence to your show, then it matters, regardless of the venue or platform. And it translates back to excitement on the court or field, no matter how the journey started.

Chapter Ten

Sportscasting Boot Camps

.

While sportscasters should feel obligated to know their own team roster, that is not enough. Especially when you are the lead broadcaster of the team on radio, television, or livestream. You are there to be the honed expert and experience in the room for the fan. And as the lead, you should feel a sense of duty to know the other team's roster coming into the venue. This goes beyond yielding a few factoids, the coach's name, or the team's win-loss record. You should want to strive in the arena of improving your overall sportscasting game. This comes by knowing about the opposing team's roster, including different aspects of the players, coaches, etc.

A lot of sportscasters have become truly lazy in this regard. They have done so by the Don Meredith / Frank Gifford standard of Monday Night Football. The pair never studied and, along with Howard Cosell while in the booth, had to have a giant chart with a stick pointing out a player who had created action on the football field. This doesn't create a sense of being a lead broadcaster, but of a rented voice. Someone who has come in, speaks about a factoid on a player, then is gone from the stadium / arena / ballpark. When an opposing team announcer cares enough to do their homework on the other team, it shows. Imagine that a coach only prepared his / her team without knowing much about the team they were facing. What if they only practiced on what they wanted to do, rather than what the team they were facing was likely to do? That would be laughed at, because the result would not be a winning strategy. The same goes for sportscasting. Knowing your team is great, but you should really have already studied up on your team over the past few weeks, months, or seasons. But what you know about that opposing team can make the overall difference in your sportscast.

Remember that you at in a weird bubble. You are the entertainment voice for the fans who are listening to you either through streaming audio/video, or by radio/television. They are looking for you to know how to break down the other team's offense/defense, beyond the generic play calling of pick and roll or screen attempts. You should know why these opposing teams run these plays and how successful they have been in other games, setting the stage as well as painting the picture for the audience. This becomes a little easier when considering the visual medium of video streaming or television, but also has its drawbacks. You cannot in some ways say too much or too little. You have to know the game, as well as the opposing team, in order to showcase your overall sportscasting game presentation.

It is truly imperative that if you want to be a successful sportscaster that you decide to focus. That means creating a boot camp for yourself prior to the game, in the hours ahead of doing the play-by-play. Remember when you crammed for that high school or college test? How you knew more about a subject because you went over the information, understood and engaged in each method, and built up an acumen of quality learning beyond what you did in the classroom? Well, that's sportscasting as well. The worst thing you can do is rely on your talent to get you through in sportscasting. "Talent" is also a good substitute word for "underachiever." The most talented people often stop attempting to build up their skills, and are passed by people not as talented but willing to put in the work and develop their craft enough to be better at what they do.

Talented people often skate by, making excuses because they do not see the need early to study, because of the belief they are talented enough to be better than those around them. Then, when they are surpassed by less talented people who are willing to do the work, they often cannot created the study skills or work ethic necessary to achieve the status that they originally had of the being the best. This occurs in every industry, including sports, where the guy drafted No. 1 overall tends to do less than the guy selected No. 199 in the 2000 draft. Ask any NFL coach who put in more work during their NFL career – No. 1 overall Courtney Brown to the Cleveland Browns, or No. 199 Tom Brady to the New England Patriots. There were six quarterbacks taken before Brady. Most of them didn't last in the NFL beyond a couple of years. As of 2021, Brady was the last of the entire 254 players selected in the 2000 NFL draft to be active on a team roster. He may not have been as talented as the 198 other players selected ahead of him, but Brady was willing to work harder, displaying the work ethic and emotional intelligence to adapt, thrive, and survive, and has proven that out several times over. Talent is nothing but an early indication of the ability to adapt, but it requires more of the person to focus that talent to be better. Often, talented people do not do enough to push themselves compared to those with the work ethic and drive to want to be a success.

A boot camp is a humbling experience. Because you are never done learning. You are never done focusing. You are there to bring out the show. Notice in a chapter prior, I spoke specifically about show prep. Well, this is about show prep, but also finding the negative sound space for you to do the show prep effectively. You cannot expect the rest of the world to stop moving, or to go absent with enough sound, in order for you to focus. You need to study up continually at your craft. And you need to not only do the research, but have the space available to make enough noise to do a sportscast run-through. This means voicing out, several times, the pronunciations of each player's first and last name. It means driving your words by reading phonically, until it makes sense. If there are issues with the opposing team, statistics, injuries, you should know that instinctive beyond the show prep. That means repeating certain facts vocally so that you know them, like a stand-up comedian does, so it sounds naturally when you repeat them during the actual sportscast. That is how a boot camp works – by focusing.

THE SPORTSCASTER'S NOTEBOOK

Your boot camp starts by finding a spare room. You could do it in a hotel room on the road. If you are doing the sportscast by yourself, you need to be alone in the room. You need to close and lock the door. Hide away from the world. Begin and trust the process. This is required of you a few hours before each game that you are handing as a sportscaster. If you have platform content issues, get those scheduled or out of the way. **Turn off the cell phone. Do not accept visitors. This is your time, your space, where you need to focus.** And when you do so, you need to be able to talk **out loud**. You need to be able to **repeat** names, sentences, factoids on the opposing team. You need know how each play will break down, and what that means for how the offense or defense will handle it. **Do not take these tasks lightly.**

No one will understand what you are doing because they do not live the life that you do. They are not there as a focused individual attempting to bring a sportscast to the world through audio or video. They are going to see your methodology as crazy. But this is because the way that you present something during a sportscast needs to sound effortless. Often people think of sportscasting as "winging it" on the air, as if that is the way that a broadcaster performs their craft. The easier that something looks, the more preparation exists ahead of time that no one sees.

This is similar to the belief that an audience has about stand-up comedians, where they believe the comedians are coming up with the words and jokes on the fly while in front of an audience. While there may be some small "writing" coming out while a comedian is on stage, the majority of the craft is developed long before. In sessions where not only are the jokes written out, but they are re-written, verbalized, honed down, crafted, and re-verbalized into a better, more coherent form. Actors do table reads, then rehearse lines, then cut sentences or add information to the script, continually before a scene is filmed for a movie or a TV show. All of this presents the opportunity for a boot camp to take place. When soldiers enter into basic training, they aren't merely given a gun and told to go to war, they are re-built from scratch, with an eight-to-ten week basic training regime, everything from sleep, cardio, eating and discipline, before they are even pushed toward being put onto the field of battle. Boot camps cut out the bullshit. This is why a boot camp for a sportscaster is necessary. The last thing that a broadcaster should be eager to do is sit down at a game table and start calling the game without any preparation.

This boot camp opportunity or study session is about taking the extra time to enhance your skills, to practice, and to verbally set the tone of your voice. Not enough sportscasters take the time to really work on their vocal skills. Sure they call a game, but they do not engage with how to work their voice effectively. The late Baseball Hall of Fame announcer Dave Niehaus was a grand master at this vocal range. When the game was intense, he would actually **slow down** how he called balls and strikes. Where he would **ease off** certain words, to present the idea that the next pitch mattered. The way that you are delivering this information to the listener who is not present in the stands matters. You are painting the picture, or bringing the show, in a way that if you merely just "call the game," you are leaving out a lot of aspects of information and detail. This is about the preparation of ensuring that you know how to speak, working that microphone, where you dance around and play. If you sound like everyone else, then you will be replaced by someone else, because you won't be unique, you will be boring.

This type of boot camp mentality also works by including a color analyst in these sessions. This is where you both get the rhythm down between the two of you when it comes to the game. This is where you avoid not being on the same page and how they interact effectively. Often, when a color analyst and sportscaster merely show up and call the game, without practicing their timing ahead of the game, they sound off. There isn't enough preparation. Imagine if you had two figure skaters who were supposed to work together on the ice, and one was supposed to lift the other one, but they had never practiced the lift prior to the night of the event. Chances are, one of them is going down on the ice. If there is a two-person team, they have to get into a room, practice, and go back and forth, to ensure that they aren't sounding unprepared. The last thing that you both should want on a sportscast is to talk over each other, leave way too much dead air space, or not enough dead air space, create a fearful environment where no one knows when the other is speaking, and in the end, it becomes a mishmash, a terrible sportscast. This does nothing for the play-by-play announcer, the color analyst and certainly nothing for the fan listening/watching at home or in the car.

When this type of crap shoot sportscast occurs, it is mainly due to a lack of preparation between the sportscaster and the color analyst. One or both did not take their role seriously enough to practice. This especially occurs with color analysts, who typically show up and expect to call out how a play is broken down, but do it generically. You can hear this when they repeat themselves several times on-air and act knowledgeable when they are clearly not. Most of the color analysts are usually the focal point of criticism by fans because they are less prepared than anyone else, including a random former player interviewed during the broadcast. But that's enough about Basketball Hall of Famer and terrible color analyst Bill Walton. The moment that he prepares for what he says will be the first time and it shows. This is why being in a spare room with a focused boot camp session, where the broadcaster and color analyst can hash things out, go through the back and forth of the upcoming game, creates an engaging experience. It allows both members of the broadcast team to understand how to click, how to work together in ways that compliment themselves and each other during the broadcast, and then present that show to the listening/viewing public.

One strong recommendation is to set the tone immediately when you get into the room with the color analyst. This is a time to focus.

All outside world issues, including cell phones, need to be turned off and put away for at least 30 minutes to an hour. This also means reducing the chit chat of standard gossip that has nothing to do with the broadcast itself. Do that at another period but focus on the task at hand. There should be an agenda, led by the sportscaster, which breaks down the focal points of the upcoming sportscast. This is a standard boot camp business meeting agenda. Go down line by line – make sure that the color analyst understands their job, their role and what you need from them during the sportscast. Again, focus.

Example of a Two Person Boot Camp Approach
1. Opposing Player Names (PHONICALLY SOUND OUT).
2. Opposing Coach Name (PHONICALLY SOUND OUT).
3. Last three game stats / details of opposing team.
4. Interesting facts / feature details of opposing team.
5. Facts / feature details of opposing players stats / personal.
6. What opposing plays will we see tonight? What has worked, what hasn't?
7. How will our team react to opposing offense / defense?
8. Details about the city, arena, area of opposing team.
9. Assignments for color analyst during game / post-game interviews.
10. Assignments for play-by-play / pre-game, halftime interview, post-game.
11. Halftime interview guests / details / new commercial reads.
12. Details for color analyst on commercial reads / other aspects.
13. Criticism of last broadcsat - what can we improve upon?

Notice how both color and play-by-play are breaking down information and parceling it out on who will provide those facts or details during the broadcast. This is important. It allows play-by-play and color to segment out when each person will chat. How they will determine points in the broadcast as to avoid stepping on the toes of the other through verbal and physical cues. If the color analyst doesn't know to talk as soon as the basket clears the hoop from inbounding to the half-court line, then they may not talk at all, or they will talk during a fast break cut toward the basketball during a score, which should be solely broadcaster territory. Getting on the same page also helps the broadcaster. While the broadcaster needs to be the eyes of the broadcast, when it's a two-person team, the color analyst needs to be the mind, dissecting why things occurred and how they equal out into a greater result of the game itself.

This is also a great period in which it is important to reduce the amount of statistics, factoids and other nuggets collected so that the broadcaster knows what they should share, and what they should leave for the color analyst to give up. Otherwise, you are both sharing the same information to the listener, and it harms the overall broadcast as information is constantly repeated. Break down what will be said during each quarter, period or inning. Make sure that there is enough room for new statistics to be mentioned, as well as other ways and information to be presented to the listener. This includes ad reads during the breaks, which can be a great way to incorporate the color analyst more. And creates the opportunity of engagement between the two, as you both can bounce off of each other ways to make the read-aloud advertisement into a fun way.

Chapter Eleven

Public Address Announcing

The public address (PA) announcer position within sportscasting earns little to no love from other broadcasting positions. Yet, the PA controls the in-game narrative of the arena, ballpark or stadium. Without a PA, the game is less than interesting. Look at the example of the 2020 NBA season inside the Orlando "bubble" after COVID-19. No fans. No PA. No in-game entertainment. It felt like a morgue holding a funeral. There is something to the aspect of being energized by the voice over the loud speaker. The crowd gets it when the PA is into it. I am not speaking of the common narrative, which suggests that a PA is a droll, dispassionate methodology for weak broadcasters or amateur hour announcers to be handed a microphone. As even high schools become more entertainment-focused, the PA announcer is now one of the hotter components of the venue experience. Sure, it isn't broadcasting over a platform that is heard by anyone outside the venue, but it matters. Again, it controls the overall in-game narrative of those who attend your games. Plus, it is an opportunity for a role with a team. Treat it with passion and grace.

Everything that the PA does from the second that they turn on the microphone matters. Everyone on the court and everyone in the stands hears it. And a great PA can make or break a game's tempo. I've witnessed a bad PA or two in my time. They can totally eliminate the in-game rhythm of the teams playing on the court or field. Mainly because of the attention that they get from what they say or don't say. There is a vibe witnessed there once someone opens up the loud speakers with a bellowing comment. It is a positive or negative vibe that generates from the PA because it can amplify and control the crowd energy, which affects the players as well as their performance.

A great compliment for any PA is how the attendees respond to you, especially when they are on the losing side of the contest. Where they clap and laugh with the PA because it is entertaining action. There is a qualifier there. You should always treat the opposing fans with a decent amount of respect. That means not being negative, especially when doing PA for high school games. Remember that these are kids. They are going to make mistakes on the court. Their families are in the crowd. This isn't a time to use words that are divisive, such as "rejection" or "denied" when a blocked shot on the opposition occurs. That wins you no fans, no interest from the opposing side.

Your job is not to antagonize the opposition or their visiting fans by using the PA as a weapon. Especially when they are down on the scoreboard. That is not your job at all. No good can come of it. Word of mouth about the job that you are doing spreads when you are having fun. That's when you are creating an overall game experience. Sure, the home team may get a bit better announcement when they do well compared to the visitors, but that isn't an excuse to be a jerk of dead air when the visitors do anything right. You have to bring an "unexpected show" where people in the crowd didn't attend because of the PA but ended up being entertained because of what the PA brings to the table.

The way that the PA talks over the microphone builds or jettisons energy with every phrase. You can gather this from standard announcements prior to the game starting, or the player intros that are delivered. The home team gets the PA charging them up, while the away team gets a lackluster introduction or a bit of a sourpuss utterance which can reflect on how the fans in the stands react as the players are announced. Think about also how scores are presented. Beyond the homerun calls, this is about the balls and strikes aspect, the meat and potatoes of being engaged so that you can keep the crowd engaged all of the time. The PA is the energy that lights up the sky within the venue in a way that other sportscasters could only dream of.

And yet, the PA announcer is often a disregarded position within sportscasting. It is not viewed on the same level as the rest of the sportscasting team. Sure, they are connecting with an in-arena audience, but other play-by-play announcers wave off comparisons to themselves and the PA. Because the PA, until the last twenty or so years, has been nothing more than a bad actor on the microphone. That has changed as generational attitudes toward in-game music have also changed. Gone are the days of having the volume at a low level, with 1970s hits playing over the loud speaker, and a droll PA announcer calling merely a foul, a player name, or an update on an out-of-town score. As Generation X and Millennials started becoming the attendees of sporting events, they wanted a vibe to keep the attention going similar to a video game. You have to hold their attention or it's lost forever. This is not necessarily a bad thing when it comes to how the PA is used in-game.

Great PA skills are borne of the opportunity of treating one-liners like music lyrics. They use them in a creative way that motivates the crowd to be a part of the action that you have created. This is like a concert of words. Keep in mind, you also have the ability to utilize sound effects and music with your one-liners. A great PA will have about six thousand one-liners loaded into their phone with a ready-made arsenal of verbal magic. Simply stating on the PA that every three-point shot made is from "downtown" is not only lazy craft but also repetitive. Sometimes, you have to be willing to state that the player is "hotter than fish grease" or made a "double-dutch, two-step call" when that player commits a travel. None of these one-liners talk down about a player on the court. The one-liners describe a piece of the action without disrespecting the player in the action.

None of your one-liners should be used more than once a game. That's because they are one-liners. And don't force it. Don't feel you have to use everything if the opportunity doesn't arise. You need to make sure that you verbalize your one-liner weaponry in a way that amazes the fans instead of overloading them. You should have a list of them, ready to go, to where you can pop them off the top of your head. Make it a show for the audience. Make them amazed at hearing how you talk about a player driving down the lane with a dunk, stating "oh, you're a mean one, mister grinch." These types of comments are what are going to drive your verbal action over the loud speakers and cause people to stay entertained beyond the game on the court itself.

Sure, the sportscaster gets to use their microphone to connect to an audience listening to an audio or video broadcast of the game. But the PA earns their immediate vote back from the audience in terms of a reaction to what they say, along with the associated marketing music that is played over the loud speakers. The PA is the hometown crowd homer at the game. They don't have to be fair or nice. They can ensure that the environment is a bit feisty for the opposing team. And that is part of the show. There is a difference between a frothy homerish environment led by the PA and being disrespectful as well. At no time should anyone on the court feel that they are being mistreated or disrespected personally. This comes back to the festive abuse factor. If everyone's not in on the joke, well, then it's not really that funny, so temper as the PA how you react to what you say. If you would be personally offended if someone referred to you by name-calling directly "i.e. look at that loser's error" comments, well, you should refrain from doing that to the players. At the end of the day, the opposing players did show up and they are part of the show as well.

That being said, as the PA, you can have fun with the homerish calls over the PA. Especially when a referee call goes the wrong way and is blatant. Nothing says that the PA cannot lead the charge of questioning that call, simply by stating "Foul on... No. 32... ???" Notice that the end of that statement becomes the question. It drives a motivating factor for the audience to also see that foul going the wrong way. The PA has the rhythm of the crowd in their pocket, especially when it is time to charge the crowd forward to spark the team, such as a long three-point shot to tie the game or go ahead from 50 feet out. Nothing says that the PA cannot turn a basketball bucket into a soccer call of "GOOOOOOOOOO-AAAAAAAAA-LLLLLL" for a good twenty-second stretch. The PA should be going wild, pushing the crowd toward an amplification of energy which the players feed off of. Make no mistake, the PA is the broadcasting mascot for the entire team. What the mascot does in the stands, the PA does over the loud speakers.

As PA, you need to work in tandem with the scorekeeper and the ref. Do not make a call on the PA concerning a foul until you have the ref report it to the scorekeeper at the game table. Otherwise, you will be issuing a "Correction" over the PA loudspeakers because you got that call wrong. Three-point shots may seem easy and clear to report over the PA, except that until the referee raises their hands to identify that a three-pointer was made, a three-pointer hasn't been scored. Think about what details you are missing at the game table that the referee might be seeing. The player's foot may have been on the three-point line, thus calling it a two-point shot. If you call it over the PA as a three-point shot, but it's not, this harms your presence as a PA in general. The crowd won't trust you.

How you conduct yourself with the scorekeeper and referees is not only about professionalism but decorum. You need to work a game table effectively. That means avoiding divisive comments toward the referees themselves. The officiating crew shouldn't have to worry that the PA is going to attack them over the loudspeakers. A little homering is fine. Too much will get you a technical on the home team. There are going to be some referees who do not enjoy the PA show at all. They won't focus enough on what's happening inside that square on the court. It is up to you as PA not to provoke them and cost the home team a technical or worse. Some referees are babies and shouldn't be officiating, yet they are. So deal with it. And kill them with kindness.

So, let's begin at the needs of the PA for the team itself. From the moment that the venue is opened up to fans, even if it's only a small group of early birds entering an arena of 5,000 empty seats, the PA needs to be active, wild and ready. Welcoming each of the fans in, really getting engaged as soon as possible. The PA also needs to function well with the marketing music in-venue. Treat this much like a play-by-play announcer and color analyst working together. Both have to understand the timing of the other. This includes later on, when sound effects are added. The last thing that either the marketing team or the PA should want is to step on the other's sound over the loud speaker, which will create nothing more than a muddled mess that no one can dissect.

The first big test of the PA announcer is the team intros. This is where the PA sets the tone for the entire game, working with the marketing staff on the team intro marketing music, style and presentation. The NBA has done an incredible job on this type of fan energy. They have traditionally turned the tables by starting the team intros with the home team first, then the opposing away team. Why? Because they black out the lights, they get the crowd moving with the home team, then they punish the away opposing team by flipping on the lights, rattling off the names accordingly but without much interest, then get into the game's events.

The PA needs to say each of the names of the players, including the opposing team players, phonically and accurately. Despite the home team players earning mega marketing introductions, stretched out by the PA and music, that doesn't mean that the opposing teams do not deserve respect. Their names should be **pronounced accurately**. They should feel that they were treated well, although their introductions were done with the lights on, no marketing music, and as efficiently or quickly as possible. That being said, it doesn't mean that during the intro, it isn't a verbal war of removing energy from the opposing team by not giving them as much of the show as the PA provides the home team. There has to be a stark difference. The PA needs to amp up the home team for the crowd, then pull back that energy from the opposing team. The home team has earned the extra juice, marketing music, and fan energy when their names are being called during the pre-game intro. The opposing team earns the crowd boos during their pre-game introduction by default while their names are read off with the speed of the roadrunner. The PA controls the crowd's overall vibe, energy, response, and expectation of the game's allure in ways that the radio / television broadcast team cannot. This is the way.

Remember that no one cares about the PA until a player's name is mispronounced over the loudspeakers. Then, everyone cares. It also shows immediately whether you are taking the matter seriously enough to work hard at your sportscasting craft. Your job is to check over the rosters ahead of time. Not only for who is on the roster, but who might have been left off but could play in the game. This will occur all of the time with late roster additions. Getting player names right is a big factor in winning at the PA. You should avoid also having an attitude if a family member or friend from the stands comes over to correct you on how the player's name is said. They are trying to help so avoid letting your ego get the best of you. Never ask a coach on how to pronounce their player's name either: They're usually not correct either.

It is smart to approach the players while they are getting warmed up to ask about name pronunciations. Be police and ask them, "excuse me, how to do you say your first or last name?" When this occurs, repeat back their name a couple of times, to ensure that you are saying their name correctly. If they have a nickname, they'll tell you as well, and potentially want you to use the nickname over their given first and last name. One kid asked that he be referred to as "air." The thing is, they gave themselves the nickname. You didn't assign the players the nickname. This is about the players feeling respected, as with the family in the stands, during the entire experience.

Let's start with how the PA can change the momentum or narrative of the game's tempo itself. If the home team is having a great run, every time that the home team scores, it can be repeated two, three times by the PA: "TWO POINTS. THAT'S TWO POINTS." This keeps the crowd engaged. Now let's say that the home team is having a dry spell, that the buckets aren't dropping, that's when the PA focused on defense or rebounding done by the home team: "REBOUND. ANOTHER SHOT COMING." The home team's effort is what matters. It engages the crowd in a way that keeps the fans interested with anticipation. The PA can also do this by ignoring when the opposing team scores where nothing is mentioned or where the PA refers to each away opposing team bucket as a "LUCKY SHOT. ALL LUCK." This helps channel the vibe for the crowd to stay active. Everything is about pulling the rabbit out of the hat, several times, to shock and awe the crowd, but keep them focused on the game itself.

But PA must and should go beyond the basic. PA should be a constant improvement of their own commentary. They need to roll with the vibe that they are creating, but update their phrasing so they aren't repeating themselves constantly. This is about playful fun with the live game environment. Whether that be on the court / field or with the fans in the stands. Yes, everything is fair game for the PA. And that is where a great PA will have a consistent message and an arsenal of comments that they can repeat throughout the season. This not only engages fans, but also allows them to get prepared for and look forward to those comments over the loud speakers.

"GIVE THAT FAN A CONTRACT" was a constant line from the late Baltimore Orioles legendary PA Rex Barney who entertained Oriole fans from 1969 to his death in 1997. He would say that "contract" line every time that a fan would make an amazing catch of a foul ball or a home run ball in the stands. And the crowd loved it. "GIVE THAT FAN… AN ERROR" was his other consistent line, when a fan would drop a foul ball or home run ball in the stands. This comes back to the terminology of festive abuse: It is not there to actually harm someone with the comment. It is to get the entire group energized around a joke that everyone is in. The legendary late comedian Don Rickles (1926-2017) was famous for his festive abuse. He would criticize himself, other newsworthy folks, and even the crowd. But none of it was made to harm someone directly and when everyone is in on the joke, it generates a laughter that is heartfelt and more entertaining. No one got upset when Rex Barney's "ERROR" comment was directed at their lack of skills catching a foul ball in the stands. In fact, a lot of the fans loved it so much, that it encouraged those fans to try to catch more foul balls or home run balls, in order to be a part of the fun. Over-sensitive people should stay home and let the rest of the crowd enjoy what they cannot: **A good time together.**

The PA is sometimes the last line of defense for a home team when the play on the court / field is terrible. When the play on the field is terrible or the team is consistently behind in the score or standings, the PA serves as the fans with the loudest bullhorn. The PA needs to know how weld that power. They start the chants, they make the comments over the loud speakers with "WHAT THE HECK?!?" and they become the show, when the game itself is boring and not entertaining otherwise. The PA also can develop their creative writing skills with different takes on commercial scripts, announcements of upcoming games, and different comments throughout the entire venue experience. The stolid, disinteresting, lack of motivated PA is dead as a position. No one wants that now. Fans want energy and excitement in today's sports world. Fans require that PAs are part of the overall show when they come to the venue. If you as a PA don't bring the show each and every time you let that microphone go hot, well, then you aren't doing anything but filling up dead space with boring information.

When the lights hit you for the first time while doing PA, it can be awestruck for you. But you have to suck it up and be ready to go. The thing is, if you are boring as a PA, you are done. If you have a bad game, you should also have a short memory otherwise it will affect you all day long. You need to **reset, process, and adjust.** Figure out a way not to do that same bad game again. Don't let it mess with you.

The thing is, as long as you can do a basic PA job, without repeating yourself, and offer a bit of pep in your voice, you will do fine. But there comes a point when you have to decide whether you want to invest the time to get better at what you are doing. Make it a show that matters, that people talk about, even when the game stinks.

A lot of organizations take for granted the duties of the PA. Until they experience a truly bad PA with a hot mic. This isn't just the standard of mentioning who is in, who scored, but really about the entire game energy itself. Marketing is built on folks getting exciting. And when the crowd isn't on their feet, it's really up to the public address announcer to get them to do so. This also follows that when it is time for moments of silence or remembrance, the public address announcer tends to slow down the pace, curb the mood. There is a solace to how their voice tempers the crowd, allowing for the ceremony to go forward in a respectful fashion. Plus, it's a job. You want to make it in sportscasting, you have to find the jobs that are open and hiring. PA is a way to not only break in, but stay in, and potentially move up to a play-by-play position. Or you might find that you can truly have more fun on a hot mic in the arena as the PA for the long-term.

A lot of PA jobs for high school games aren't really sought after because the school districts often delay pay until the next month. There's also the inability for schools to decipher between folks willing to do PA for free who are horrible compared to a skilled professional who takes the position seriously. There is a certain bonus though out of being a PA for high school games, because there are a lot of tournaments, including the state tournaments, where you can shine. It all comes down to whether you bring a rhythm to your overall sportscasting skill set. Do you take the PA job as serious as a play-by-play broadcast? You should bring the flavor to the game. You should have a relationship with your fellow PA folks. Get the game scores ahead of time. Preparation and investment help you bring the show to another level. Sure, no one walked into the gym to see you, but they will remember a great show if you provide it. Especially if their team went from sugar to shit.

Chapter Twelve

Creating
A
Radio / TV Magazine Show

A large missing piece for extra broadcast work assignments comes in the form of a recap or magazine show for radio/television. It is referred to as a magazine show because it is not live, and more of an update of the sports landscape and the team's place within it, in a general format of 30 minutes to one hour. The magazine show is much different than a coaches show, which is less on pre-recorded material and more focused on live interviews of coaches and players, with a strict adherence to the format wheel time clock to hit each break. Those tend to be less difficult to do. But a radio/television magazine show is much different and much more difficult. These are broken down into various segments with pre-taped interviews or highlights, long before they air to the public in their time slot.

Radio/television magazine shows have been around for decades. Not just in sports either. Several national AM/FM radio classic rock music stations play the magazine show "Breakfast with the Beatles" on Sunday mornings as filler material, with different hosts talking up each segment of the programming. "Breakfast with the Beatles" is about selling nostalgia beyond all else, airing lost or historical audio interviews, songs, and variations of songs that weren't released as part of the original album. They will also do "this date in history" components, tying it into what the Beatles were up to on a tour or in a studio session. This creates a continued interest in not only the Beatles, but of listeners tuning in each weekend to hear where the band from Britain, which broke up in 1970, shows relevancy to today's musical landscape.

Your team's own magazine show can exist on a smaller scale than the Beatles. Even if it's for one local radio/television station rather than an entire worldwide network, the magazine show can gain a set listener following. Magazine shows have many of the same aspects as the "Breakfast with the Beatles" show. The show is able to set the narrative by bringing fans closer to the art of the game while being cheap and easy to produce. Often, the sports magazine shows are clips of past interviews, historical facts, and some highlights. And they can be packaged into a 30-minute or hour-long program that houses several commercial breaks. This is where you as the broadcaster can embed different interview styles, honing your craft, while creating expanded clips, for a newsletter subscription later on. All of this feeds back into the idea of knowing what you are trying to accomplish.

42:00 - Third Segment Intro Package (0:12)
42:13 - Host Show Intro No. 3 (0:35)
42:48 - Tease Upcoming Team Schedule Package (3:00)
45:48 - Current Team Standings Package (0:30)
46:18 - Final Segment Interview (8:00)
54:18 - Social Media Reminder Package (0:30)
54:48 - Sponsor Thank Package No. 3 (0:30)
55:18 - Host Show Outro No. 3 (0:50)
56:08 - Show Credits Package (0:12)

0:00 - Intro Package (0:13)
0:13 - Host Show Intro No. 1 (0:35)
0:48 - Highlight Package No. 1 (2:30)
3:18 - League Stand Package (3:30)
6:48 - Host Segment / Social No. 1 (0:30)
7:18 - Highlight Package No. 2 (6:00)
13:18 - Sponsor Thank Package No. 1 (2:00)
15:18 - BIG Interview Teaser (1:30)
17:18 - Host Segment Outro No. 1 (1:42)

22:30 - Second Segment Intro Package (0:13)
22:43 - Host Show Intro No. 2 (0:35)
23:12 - BIG Interview Segment No. 1 (12:00)
35:12 - Final Segment Interview Teaser (1:30)
36:18 - Sponsor Thank Package No. 2 (1:30)
37:48 - Host Segment Outro No. 2 (1:12)

The first component of any magazine show is to tease a big interview that will be played during the program. This interview can be of a player, coach, or former player, someone of larger interest to the listeners. This type of teasing comes for the first 25 minutes of the program, where small snippets of interview quotes are sprinkled throughout the program. During the first 25 minutes of the program, there should be segments on the past week's game highlights, so that you are catching up fans who are listening/watching, along with providing an entire worldview of the team's current position in the league standings. Then, you go into the interview itself, which should be less than 10 minutes, while teasing that those listeners who subscribe to the Patreon newsletter can gain access to the expanded interview. This creates incentive for your followers to do what you are asking of them. The rest of the program should be a preparation for the week ahead for the team, including with a regular guest such as a sports journalist, in pre-recorded fashion. All of this is to tease the listener/ viewer not only to continue supporting the program, but to also be entertained enough to see the team in a live setting.

The entire program should be viewed in a pattern. You should be able to set up key points in visual/audio editing in order to hit set commercial breaks. This should be easy to produce, driving home the idea of initiating a highlight clip from a game, breaking down a segment, and including the interview portion which can be filmed and edited in the weeks prior to the airing of the magazine show.

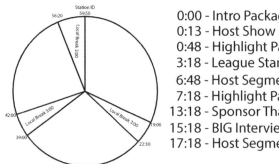

0:00 - Intro Package (0:13)
0:13 - Host Show Intro No. 1 (0:35)
0:48 - Highlight Package No. 1 (2:30)
3:18 - League Stand Package (3:30)
6:48 - Host Segment / Social No. 1 (0:30)
7:18 - Highlight Package No. 2 (6:00)
13:18 - Sponsor Thank Package No. 1 (2:00)
15:18 - BIG Interview Teaser (1:30)
17:18 - Host Segment Outro No. 1 (1:42)

And some of the highlights can be re-edited after each game from 10-15 minutes down to small 3-minute clips, making it easier to compile for the highlight portion. The journalist regular guest interview on the backend can be done right after the last game has been completed that week, while the entire venue is being shut down for the night. All of it can be straight back-and-forth to capture what is needed, which is a preview of the team's upcoming schedule. All of this should fit within the time clock pattern of the magazine show, and should become easier to initiate as you get the flow down efficiently.

Right now, some of those reading this are asking why they should want to do a magazine show. They have enough duties, enough things on their plate. But this is part of a bigger scheme for your sportscasting career. It allows you to have a larger resume builder for future jobs and provides the team with the ability to offer up more content to their viewers. It is a win-win. When another team paying more money asks you for additional clips, having several interviews or a magazine show to choose from may be the determining factor in your getting the job.

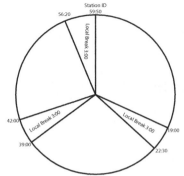

22:30 - Second Segment Intro Package (0:13)
22:43 - Host Show Intro No. 2 (0:35)
23:12 - BIG Interview Segment No. 1 (12:00)
35:12 - Final Segment Interview Teaser (1:30)
36:18 - Sponsor Thank Package No. 2 (1:30)
37:48 - Host Segment Outro No. 2 (1:12)

Everything is about putting the work in for later. If you don't put in the work now, with something that entices future employers to see the mountain of skill in editing, interviewing, and engagement that you can provide their listeners, you may not be viewed as tangible enough to hire. Simple as that.

42:00 - Third Segment Intro Package (0:12)
42:13 - Host Show Intro No. 3 (0:35)
42:48 - Tease Upcoming Team Schedule Package (3:00)
45:48 - Current Team Standings Package (0:30)
46:18 - Final Segment Interview (8:00)
54:18 - Social Media Reminder Package (0:30)
54:48 - Sponsor Thank Package No. 3 (0:30)
55:18 - Host Show Outro No. 3 (0:50)
56:08 - Show Credits Package (0:12)

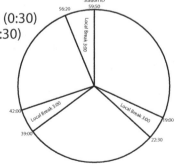

Evergreen Content Recorded / Edited Months Prior to Air

0:00 - Intro Package (0:13)
6:48 - Host Segment / Social No. 1 (0:30)
13:18 - Sponsor Thank Package No. 1 (2:00)
22:30 - Second Segment Intro Package (0:13)
36:18 - Sponsor Thank Package No. 2 (1:30)
42:00 - Third Segment Intro Package (0:12)
54:18 - Social Media Reminder Package (0:30)
54:48 - Sponsor Thank Package No. 3 (0:30)
56:08 - Show Credits Package (0:12)

Recorded / Edited Three Weeks Prior to Air

0:13 - Host Show Intro No. 1 (0:35)
15:18 - BIG Interview Teaser (1:30)
17:18 - Host Segment Outro No. 1 (1:42)
22:43 - Host Show Intro No. 2 (0:35)
23:12 - BIG Interview Segment No. 1 (12:00)
37:48 - Host Segment Outro No. 2 (1:12)
42:13 - Host Show Intro No. 3 (0:35)
42:48 - Tease Upcoming Team Schedule Package (3:00)
55:18 - Host Show Outro No. 3 (0:50)

Recorded / Edited Week Prior to Air

0:48 - Highlight Package No. 1 (2:30)
3:18 - League Stand Package (3:30)
7:18 - Highlight Package No. 2 (6:00)
35:12 - Final Segment Interview Teaser (1:30)
45:48 - Current Team Standings Package (0:30)
46:18 - Final Segment Interview (8:00)

Chapter Thirteen

Developing
A
Commercial Log System

Ignorance of a commercial log system is unacceptable in today's age of media and sponsorship. If you refuse to read this section, blow it off as unimportant to you, or decline to develop a commercial log system yourself, then you will likely fail as a sportscaster. This is the meat and potatoes of the back end of the sportscasting game. The commercial log system is a variant. It is not required to match the log system found in this book completely, but the ones provided here should be treated as a starting point for those who wish to present a professional broadcast. The commercial log system isn't simply for commercials either. It is also to protect your voice, preventing you from over-extension by talking throughout the entire 2-3 hours of the sports contest by providing much needed breaks.

Basketball Game Commercial Log
Date_____   Opponent _____
I hereby certify that the commercials listed aired at the times listed (name of announcer)_____ Date _____

Segment	Break #	Spot Title	Length	Client	Time Aired	Initial
Pregame	LIVE	Pregame Intro	:20	LIVE	_____	_____
Pregame	#1	Station ID	:10	Inhouse	_____	_____
Pregame	#1	**SPONSOR**	:30	**AD**	_____	_____
Pregame	LIVE	Lineup/Matchup	2:00	LIVE	_____	_____
Pregame	#2	**SPONSOR**	:30	**AD**	_____	_____
Pregame	#2	**SPONSOR**	:60	**AD**	_____	_____
Pregame	TAPE	Coaches Corner	2:00	Inhouse	_____	_____
Pregame	#3	**SPONSOR**	:30	**AD**	_____	_____
Pregame	#3	**SPONSOR**	:30	**AD**	_____	_____
Pregame	#3	**SPONSOR**	:30	**AD**	_____	_____
Pregame	#3	**SPONSOR**	:30	**AD**	_____	_____
Pregame	TAPE	Player Interview	2:00	Inhouse	_____	_____
Pregame	#4	**SPONSOR**	:60	**AD**	_____	_____
Pregame	#4	**SPONSOR**	:30	**AD**	_____	_____
Pregame	LIVE	Wrapup Pre	2:00	LIVE	_____	_____
Pregame	#5	**SPONSOR**	:60	**AD**	_____	_____
Pregame	#5	**SPONSOR**	:30	**AD**	_____	_____
Pregame	#5	**SPONSOR**	:30	**AD**	_____	_____
Pregame	TAPE	Pregame Out	:20	Inhouse	_____	_____
Pregame	#5	Station ID	:10	Inhouse	_____	_____

Commercial logs were developed as a way to help the advertiser confirm that their sponsorship spots were being run and at what time. The system, if not used, will force your broadcast to sound unprofessional and haphazard. Thus, do not expect a ton of sponsorship if you refuse to confirm that the spots ran and at what time during the game.

It comes with the territory as a sportscaster that you develop a commercial game log system, then send copies back to the station or mail them out to your sponsors. This is a way to confirm to sponsors that you indeed ran their advertisements, that you were honest and attempted like hell to get every sponsor's advertisement in on time, etc.

Newspapers perform a similar method with a practice called "tear sheets" in which they mail directly to their sponsors the newspaper advertisements which were run. So if you were hesitant in developing a commercial log system, think again. Everyone does it for a specific reason – to get paid.

Men's Basketball Game Commercial Log
Date_____   Opponent _____
I hereby certify that the commercials listed aired at the times listed (name of announcer)_____ Date _____

Segment	Break #	Spot Title	Length	Client	Time Aired	Initial
Pregame	LIVE	Pregame Intro	:20	LIVE	_____	_____
Pregame	#1	Station ID	:10	Inhouse	_____	_____
Pregame	#1	**SPONSOR**	:30	**AD**	_____	_____
Pregame	LIVE	Lineup/Matchup	2:00	LIVE	_____	_____
Pregame	#2	**SPONSOR**	:30	**AD**	_____	_____
Pregame	#2	**SPONSOR**	:60	**AD**	_____	_____
Pregame	TAPE	Coaches Corner	2:00	Inhouse	_____	_____
Pregame	#3	**SPONSOR**	:30	**AD**	_____	_____
Pregame	#3	**SPONSOR**	:30	**AD**	_____	_____
Pregame	#3	**SPONSOR**	:30	**AD**	_____	_____
Pregame	#3	**SPONSOR**	:30	**AD**	_____	_____
Pregame	TAPE	Player Interview	2:00	Inhouse	_____	_____
Pregame	#4	**SPONSOR**	:60	**AD**	_____	_____
Pregame	#4	**SPONSOR**	:30	**AD**	_____	_____
Pregame	LIVE	Wrapup Pre	2:00	LIVE	_____	_____
Pregame	#5	**SPONSOR**	:60	**AD**	_____	_____
Pregame	#5	**SPONSOR**	:30	**AD**	_____	_____
Pregame	#5	**SPONSOR**	:30	**AD**	_____	_____
Pregame	TAPE	Pregame Out	:20	Inhouse	_____	_____
Pregame	#5	Station ID	:10	Inhouse	_____	_____

THE SPORTSCASTER'S NOTEBOOK

The pregame log really sets up your broadcast from the start. Notice that in this log for the pregame, you have exactly 12 sponsorship spots to fill as well as run. Three of those spots are also 60 seconds.

This also helps guide you in a format with the pregame show in general so that things are presented evenly without any opportunity to get out of hand. It gives you structure as to when the lineups need to be read, when the taped interviews with the coach and player are going to be broadcast, and which sponsors are run at which times. As stated earlier in Chapter Ten, sponsors like to be married around certain events or levels when they believe that listeners will be paying attention the most.

This pregame schedule is set for 15 minutes prior to tip-off. Unless you are a professional organization with a large listenership, as well as have the opportunity for multiple guests and call-in listeners, it is best to stay within a 15-minute start-up window. Otherwise, things get out of hand quick and you end up with bad or dead air.

Halftime is where your feet get put to the fire. If you cease to have a good show and the game appears to be lopsided, you will drop listeners quickly. This is not good for the broadcast, for retention of sponsors, and for your future endeavors as a sportscaster. The best way to prevent all of those bad to worse scenarios from happening is to develop a good halftime commercial game log.

Notice that the stats and synopsis of the first half are presented

Basketball Game Commercial Log
Date_____   Opponent _____
I hereby certify that the commercials listed aired at the times listed (name of announcer)_____ Date _____

Segment	Break #	Spot Title	Length	Client	Time Aired	Initial
1st Half	#1	SPONSOR	:60	AD	_____	_____
1st Half	#2	SPONSOR	:30	AD	_____	_____
1st Half	#2	SPONSOR	:30	AD	_____	_____
1st Half	#3	SPONSOR	:30	AD	_____	_____
1st Half	#3	SPONSOR	:30	AD	_____	_____
1st Half	#4	SPONSOR	:60	AD	_____	_____
1st Half	#5	SPONSOR	:30	AD	_____	_____
1st Half	#5	SPONSOR	:30	AD	_____	_____
1st Half	#6	SPONSOR	:30	AD	_____	_____
1st Half	#6	SPONSOR	:30	AD	_____	_____
1st Half	#7	SPONSOR	:30	AD	_____	_____
1st Half	#7	SPONSOR	:30	AD	_____	_____
1st Half	#8	SPONSOR	:60	AD	_____	_____
1st Half	#9	SPONSOR	:60	AD	_____	_____
1st Half	#10	SPONSOR	:30	AD	_____	_____
1st Half	#10	SPONSOR	:30	AD	_____	_____

Basketball Game Commercial Log
Date_____   Opponent _____
I hereby certify that the commercials listed aired at the times listed (name of announcer)_____ Date _____

Segment	Break #	Spot Title	Length	Client	Time Aired	Initial
2nd Half	#1	SPONSOR	:60	AD	_____	_____
2nd Half	#2	SPONSOR	:30	AD	_____	_____
2nd Half	#2	SPONSOR	:30	AD	_____	_____
2nd Half	#3	SPONSOR	:30	AD	_____	_____
2nd Half	#4	SPONSOR	:60	AD	_____	_____
2nd Half	#5	SPONSOR	:30	AD	_____	_____
2nd Half	#5	SPONSOR	:30	AD	_____	_____
2nd Half	#6	SPONSOR	:30	AD	_____	_____
2nd Half	#7	SPONSOR	:30	AD	_____	_____
2nd Half	#8	SPONSOR	:60	AD	_____	_____
2nd Half	#9	SPONSOR	:60	AD	_____	_____
2nd Half	#10	SPONSOR	:30	AD	_____	_____
2nd Half	#10	SPONSOR	:30	AD	_____	_____

Basketball Game Commercial Log
Date_____   Opponent _____
I hereby certify that the commercials listed aired at the times
listed (name of announcer)_____ Date _____

Segment	Break #	Spot Title	Length	Client	Time Aired	Initial
Halftime	LIVE	Halftime Intro	:20	LIVE	_____	____
Halftime	#1	Station ID	:10	Inhouse	_____	____
Halftime	#1	**SPONSOR**	:30	**AD**	_____	____
Halftime	LIVE	Stats/Synopsis	2:00	LIVE	_____	____
Halftime	#2	**SPONSOR**	:30	**AD**	_____	____
Halftime	#2	**SPONSOR**	:60	**AD**	_____	____
Halftime	TAPE	Athlete of Week	2:00	Inhouse	_____	____
Halftime	#3	**SPONSOR**	:30	**AD**	_____	____
Halftime	#3	**SPONSOR**	:30	**AD**	_____	____
Halftime	#3	**SPONSOR**	:30	**AD**	_____	____
Halftime	#3	**SPONSOR**	:30	**AD**	_____	____
Halftime	TAPE	Interview	2:00	Inhouse	_____	____
Halftime	#4	**SPONSOR**	:60	**AD**	_____	____
Halftime	#4	**SPONSOR**	:30	**AD**	_____	____
Halftime	LIVE	Wrapup Halftime	2:00	LIVE	_____	____
Halftime	#5	**SPONSOR**	:60	**AD**	_____	____
Halftime	#5	**SPONSOR**	:30	**AD**	_____	____

Basketball Game Commercial Log
Date_____   Opponent _____
I hereby certify that the commercials listed aired at the times
listed (name of announcer)_____ Date _____

Segment	Break #	Spot Title	Length	Client	Time Aired	Initial
Postgame	LIVE	Postgame Intro	:20	LIVE	_____	____
Postgame	#1	Station ID	:10	Inhouse	_____	____
Postgame	#1	**SPONSOR**	:30	**AD**	_____	____
Postgame	LIVE	Synopsis/Recap	2:00	LIVE	_____	____
Postgame	#2	**SPONSOR**	:30	**AD**	_____	____
Postgame	#2	**SPONSOR**	:60	**AD**	_____	____
Postgame	LIVE	Coach Interview	2:00	LIVE	_____	____
Postgame	#3	**SPONSOR**	:30	**AD**	_____	____
Postgame	#3	**SPONSOR**	:30	**AD**	_____	____
Postgame	#3	**SPONSOR**	:30	**AD**	_____	____
Postgame	LIVE	Player Interview	2:00	LIVE	_____	____
Postgame	#4	**SPONSOR**	:60	**AD**	_____	____
Postgame	#4	**SPONSOR**	:30	**AD**	_____	____
Postgame	LIVE	Wrapup Post	2:00	LIVE	_____	____
Postgame	#5	**SPONSOR**	:60	**AD**	_____	____
Postgame	#5	**SPONSOR**	:30	**AD**	_____	____

first. This is to help listeners grasp what details have happened in the game and how the game has developed. This is especially true if you are broadcasting an event where there is a record or some important information happening in the game.

This mission with the halftime show is to blend the LIVE broadcast with taped interviews. If you can get a LIVE interview, that is great, however, that likely will not happen as often as you would like or hope.

Because both the first half and the second half are similar in how the commercial logs are developed, they were included on one page instead of two. Both sets have varying times of 30-second and 60-second commercial spots. Generally, each timeout and break is worth about 60 seconds. Going beyond that in the game can force you to either cut the commercial short (which is not good if the sponsor listens or hears about it from someone else) or miss some of the game trying to fulfill the spot.

As you can see, there is a necessity to commercial log systems. They protect you from the advertiser who will claim that their spot didn't run because they specifically were listening to the broadcast and didn't hear it. This is a good backup to your credibility as well. It shows that you are paying attention when you run ad spots overall.

Chapter Fourteen

Show Prep
for
Sportscasting

It is required that you learn how to show prep for your program or PBP. If you want to develop a great sportscast, it starts with show prep. Even if it's a low-end game for a non-descript high school, simply calling out the plays, the score or the offense/defense doesn't cut it. You should want to know more to convey more about what your listeners tune in for. Everyone who is successful in sportscasting, whether it is sports talk or a PBP gig, has tons of hours of show prep behind their broadcast. Everyone who decides to "wing it" should everyone else, which means that they are replaceable. "Winging it" is another way to keep yourself from being successful in sportscasting.

Show Prep Binder

The best way to compile and keep your notes on everything that a PBP or sports talk show will require is a big binder. You should have the binder divided into different sections. It is also smart to have extra pens, a yellow highlighter and a note pad handy in case you need to be told something non-verbally by coaches or staff on-air that you can relay to your audience. I realize that most of you will think about logging everything into a laptop or iPad. The issue with that is that batteries can die, usually mid-game, and then you cannot access your information.

THE SPORTSCASTER'S NOTEBOOK

Show Prep Binder Sections

1. Pregame Intro

2. Game Highlights

3. Live Copy #1

4. Live Copy #2

5. Live Copy #3

6. Live Copy #4

7. Live Copy #5

8. Game Logs

9. Home Bios

10. Home Stats

11. Visitor Stats

12. Post Game/Misc.

Section - Pregame Intro: This is where your typed pregame intro goes. You should practice or go over it once or twice prior to actually saying it on the air. Voice it out loud, make sure that you are concise and can hit the beats correctly to sound coherent. Separating this from the group of information that you have in the show prep binder makes it easier to find when you are attempt to go LIVE with the broadcast. Remember, this is the opening salvo of the entire PBP. You need to draw in the attention of the listener/viewer, get them engaged with the who, what, why, when and how of this game.

Section – Game Highlights: This is where you put down any possible highlights of interest that you may mention during the game. Little tidbits or nuggets of stats. These include whether a player is approaching a 1,000 points for a season or career, rankings of the team in the conference or coaching records. You may not get to all of the highlights. But it helps because if the game becomes slow, or if there is a break in the action, you want to have more knowledge than just hitting the button to play advertisements. You want to sound credible, and having game highlights already in your binder, ready to go, will enhance the overall broadcast.

Section – Live Copy 1-5: All of your live copy goes into this section. A good suggestion is to have the live copy as it appears. This will allow you to get to that section faster without missing a beat. Again, its best to practice every live copy piece a few times before going LIVE with the broadcast. This is what your advertisers are paying for. They want to hear non-canned statements from you, during the game, to hit the listenership/viewership with during small breaks in the action. It keeps the listener/viewer tuned in, grabbing their attention.

Section – Game Logs: Placing all of your extra game log sheets in this section is where you can have backup. This is in case one of your current game logs goes missing or coffee/juice/water/liquid drenches it. No advertiser likes a game log which is coffee stained.

Section – Home/Visitor Bios: Every biography of a player and coach should be in this section. Not just the stats, but also the stupid stuff. If a player likes sailing or another one has a degree as a water technician, it matters. This separates your broadcast in those moments with the element of action has slowed or is in a standstill such as free throws.

THE SPORTSCASTER'S NOTEBOOK

Example: *"Steve Brown goes to the line for the 1-and-1. He's actually a pretty good quarters player in his spare time. Apparently, no one on his team can beat him because he just finds the glass. Brown hits the free throw on the front end of the 1-and-1, but no glass this time."*

Section – Home/Visitor Stats: You should not only have current stats for the entire year, but also the last 3 or 4 game stat sheets that both teams have played. Use a yellow highlighter and seek out those interesting stats during the last couple of games for your broadcast. When you have a chance, utilize these stats for a mention or two, especially when a bench player gets hot on the court.

Example: *"Emily Brown has been perfect tonight from the 3-point line against Xaiver. She did the same thing, two games ago, facing off with Marshall. An 11-for-11 performance behind the arch in a 102-92 victory December 13th."*

Section – Post Game/Misc: This is the section where you keep all of the extra stuff. In case you have a guest coming on, or there's a special announcement, such as the game next week is on at 3 p.m. instead of 7 p.m. This helps keep your broadcast and information organized and ready for upcoming mentions or events.

Weekly Releases

The majority of college athletic programs, including small colleges, have a sports information director (SID) assigned to handle public relations requests. If you approach them with the right amount of time, they can provide you with nearly everything on the team or information regarding the upcoming game. Sometimes, these are half-paid positions where an assistant coach or administrative assistant moonlights to cover their other half-pay position with the college. Chapter 18 covers working with the SID in more detail.

A lot of SIDs do place several key documents on their website daily, helping streamline the process of seeking out different tidbits of information. One of the necessary documents they place online is called a weekly release, which entails everything that a sportscaster could want, including quotes from the coach, stat sheets from the last two home games, and player notes.

A good rule of thumb is to look at both the home and away websites. Seek out as much information from weekly releases as possible. Both schools and newspapers should provide you with enough information to make a great sportscast show prep possible.

Example:
OMAHA FIREBALLS BASKETBALL
13-2 overall, 2-1 in conference
Weekly Notes – Jan 3, 2021

Upcoming Games: Jan. 6 vs. No. 3 Stevens Quarry (11-4, 1-1); Jan. 8 vs. No. 2 Missouri Valley Saints (15-0, 4-0).

Past Games: Nov. 3 – vs Pacific University – W, 91-49; Nov. 9 at Washington State – L, 41-68; Nov. 12 at New Mexico L, 52-92.

Fireballs ignite with five 3-point shots to get into overtime against Mississippi College, but lose in a heartbreaker, 122-121.

Gene Ain't Happy with Second Place: Head Coach Gene Upwright said that the Fireballs shouldn't accept the second place trophy at the Sydney Tournament, after the team lost to Mississippi State in a heartbreaking overtime loss.

"It just ain't us to finish second, and I don't expect our players to be comfortable with it either."

THE SPORTSCASTER'S NOTEBOOK

Other quotes from the tournament:

"We go home with a championship or we don't eat during the night after the trip,"
Gene Upwright.

"I just got into the lower corner and started making threes like there was no
tomorrow and never was a yesterday. I cooled off and let my team down during
overtime though," – John Bill, Fireballs guard.

Chapter Fifteen

Developing
Your
Writing Skills

Despite whatever your father, uncle, grandparent or friend thinks about sportscasting, it is not a business for the illiterate. Frankly, if you do not develop exceptional writing skills, you will fail at the craft of sportscasting. While some may believe that the previous statement is hard to comprehend in an industry built on verbal communication, the reality is that most of the verbal communication has been written first, then delivered orally. "Winging it" is not worth your time, nor your listeners.

Those who are successful in broadcasting know how to write. They developed their skills in writing before they developed their sportscasting. Their writing skills are comparable to that of most print/online journalists. Period. End of sentence.

Writing takes time. You have to focus each sentence. Understand how to develop it into an orally satisfying manner. Retaining the interest of the listening audience along the way. It all starts with the opening script of your pregame show. Which can make or break your broadcast.

Imagine your listening audience tuning into your broadcast, only to find the PBP stumbling around with their words, unable to really tell anyone why they should list. PA folks tend to practice, several times, speaking aloud, each of the names of the home and away players, prior to going LIVE over the public address system in the arena. That is why writing is so important. It lays out a great foundation for the rest of the broadcast, helping the talent succeed at their craft. You only get one shot at being right in a LIVE situation. It is better to write it down, practice it, before you take your one shot at success or failure.

Writing The Pregame Intro

The **Who, What, When, Where, How & Why** of journalism is applied to the opening script of your basketball pregame show. General information is brought as a teaser in order to develop why your target audience should listen.

This develops further with more information which expands the reasoning behind why this game is important, what is going on, when it will happen, the location of the game and how it will be carried out. This is a general teaser with entices the listener with the sharpest of aspects.

A good rule of thought is that you pretend you are running up to a single person and telling them what is happened. Generally, in that type of information, you would cut to the chase and tell them exactly what they need to know immediately, then expand further later. This intro portion of the pregame script is no different.

INTRO

Tonight the Simmons Bearcats boys basketball squad looks to build on the momentum of their last win against Wilson Devil Dogs. The Bearcats bring a 11-10 record into tonight's road match up and will look to climb their way back toward the top of the Metro League against the OnAlaska Wildcats. The Wildcats enter tonight's contest having lost 7 of their last 8 with a 10-7 record on the year and a 2-7 record in the conference. The Bearcats will be led tonight by Junior Orville Carlson and Senior John Rider. Long and Rider are coming off the last game which saw them score in double figures and will look to repeat that performance again tonight. On the other side of the ball, the Wildcats will be led by Ernie Waywright. The Sophomore Forward led the Wildcats in scoring in their last game here on their home court against Centralia Cyclones. All will square off tonight; LIVE in Metro League boy's basketball action here on the Bearcats Network, coming up next...

THE SPORTSCASTER'S NOTEBOOK

Writing The Pregame Open

Now you have an expanded version of the intro, which showcases far more than just a teaser. This larger edition has been made in order to take those listeners who have already been snared by your daring teaser and holds onto them with more information. This pregame open explains in-depth why they should continue listening, raises the stakes higher as to what teams are playing and how this game fits into the overall arch of the season. This entire pregame open fits the pattern of **Classic Story Structure**.

OPENING

Hello fans and welcome to the Mead Bearcats pre-game show on the Bearcats Network here at KWKY. We're glad you could join us. I'm John Doe. Tonight we come to you live from OnAlaska, Ohio where we are in a Metro League matchup between the Bearcats and Wildcats.

One year ago, Orville Carlson was sitting on the Bearcats bench with a broken leg and watched his team go down in flames against the OnAlaska Wildcats in a shootout. Back after an intense rehab throughout the summer, Orville is now atop the Metro League leaders with 20.5 points and 10.6 rebounds per game and 19 Division I offers on the table. Across the floor, he faces a McDonald's All-American candidate in OnAlaska's Ernie Waywright, who has average 35 points and 20 rebounds per contest with a 6-8 frame.

In order to stop Waywright, Bearcats coach Hans Kilk, Jr. will be will be looking for numerous players to step into roles and make things happen. The bench has depth and over the past few games has seen plenty of action. Jack Black will be looked upon to provide some defense as he has come away with 62 steals on the season. Sam Sneed will need to help knock down some three-pointers as they have in the last two games. There are plenty of players that can help and with the improved defensive play of the team they just need to overcome the slow starts. If they can jump on this Wildcat team early they should be able to keep some distance with their persistent defense.

We'll come back with coach Kilk's thoughts after this on the Bearcats Radio Network... (**cue sponsors, then canned coaches corner**).

Classic Story Structure

Classical Story Structure has been around since people first started telling stories and is used in 99 percent of all of the world's stories, including radio and film. Sportscasting typically uses **Classical Story Structure** in order to develop its storyline. Simply put, it is a format of beginning, middle, and end. The 18th century British tale of Jack & Jill is a perfect example: They go up the hill, they fall down the hill while breaking bones, they get up and go after the water again, they achieve their goal and bring the water back to mother, who thanks them. Part of **Classical Structure** is an active protagonist who must struggle against increased antagonism into order to reach an ultimate and irreversible end. Using **Classical Story Structure**, look again at the open and see how it is used to develop the storyline of the game.

Notice that we are set up with a tragedy beyond the initial story of Simmon's Orville Carlson, who is returning from an injury the previous season and is now facing a league rival. Carlson was unable to help his team last season and it resulted in the loss.

This is the first amount of antagonism presented in the storyline to the listeners (will he or won't he return to form). Now, notice the second form of antagonism, a brief description of Carlson returning to form after a summer of rehab. The third and ultimate form of antagonism which stands between Carlson and his goals comes in the form of Ernie Waywright, who seems to dominate the Metro League with his statistics and sheer size.

This sets a David vs. Goliath story, transforming a game between two schools into an ultimate showdown of essentially two characters who are fighting against each other to win. By focusing the storyline down to two characters, it intensifies the need to pay attention for the listeners.

Writing LIVE COPY

Writing LIVE copy is important. There may be events that occur where you need to make an announcement that is important to the listener, or it may be a great way to sell additional sponsorship. Thirty seconds of verbal wordage equals five or six lines of text.

Keep everything concise. Simplify the words to make sure that they are understood by the listener. You might need to practice a few times, to ensure that you give the copy a high quality read when you go LIVE with that copy. Writing in CAPS tends to also simplify the process as well. Notice that writing LIVE copy is simplistic, but gives every detail of information possible.

John's RC is at Samuel's place; it has over 50 different cars, but none of that is important. How exactly you get there, from start of the break, is important. Notice that it is a FASTBREAK timeout that you are going into. The word "FAST" is used twice to convey a relation between why the timeout was taken, and what the message means to the listener. Keep this in mind as you begin to secure sponsorship. How you use their message may be the difference between a klunky break and a good spot.

Writing A Highlight Package

When writing a highlight package, it is important to marry each of the images properly with the narration involved. Notice in the example below that each image focuses on a back and forth between Jefferies and Steves, likely set up by a LIVE introduction by the host who sets the table between the two players. The culmination is to show how close Jefferies came to success but failed, then transitions to an post-game interview with Jefferies about the game.

Example:
CLIP: Jefferies slam dunk (0:05)
NARRATOR: Stan Jefferies shows his stuff with a jam to lead the game.
CLIP: Steves Pass to Baxter, Alley-Oop (0:05)
NARRATOR: Steves answers later in the second half with an alley-oop to Baxter for 2.
CLIP: End of Game Three-Point Show Misses (0:10)
NARRATOR: And it comes down to Jefferies, two seconds left, who misses the three, losing the game.
CLIP W/ AUDIO: Jefferies talks about losing the game on a last second three point show in the locker room (0:15)

Developing A Good Flow System

This chart may help you in developing a good flow system. It is designed to mirror that of football depth charts, in order for PBP announcers to find names quickly without having to look up little pencil written names in a book during the game. It may be useful to you in terms of PBP for basketball as well, as sometimes the names can be tricky and those few seconds that you can't come up with a name on-air, you can look down and find it easy enough with this chart.

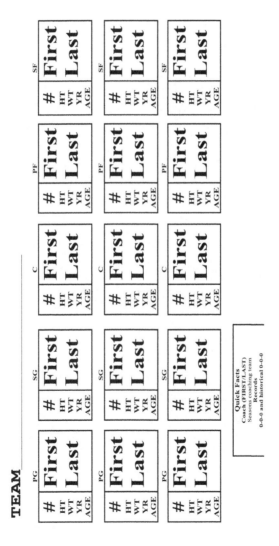

THE SPORTSCASTER'S NOTEBOOK

BASKETBALL SCORE SHEET

VISITORS _____ Uniform Color _____

Team fouls: □ 1st half `1` `2` `3` `4` `5` `6` `7` `8` `9` `10` `•`   Time Outs: □ 60 sec. `1` `2` `3`
□
□   2nd half `1` `2` `3` `4` `5` `6` `7` `8` `9` `10` `•`   □   30 sec. `1` `2`
                                    1 + 1   2 shots

No.	U	Player	Fouls					SCORING: 3 = 3 point goal 2 = 2 point goal ● = FT made ○ = FT missed			
								1st	2nd	3rd	4th
			1	2	3	4	5				
			1	2	3	4	5				
			1	2	3	4	5				
			1	2	3	4	5				
			1	2	3	4	5				
			1	2	3	4	5				
			1	2	3	4	5				
			1	2	3	4	5				
			1	2	3	4	5				
			1	2	3	4	5				
			1	2	3	4	5				
			1	2	3	4	5				
FINAL SCORE _____			Quarter Totals								

HOME _____ Uniform Color _____

Team fouls: □ 1st half `1` `2` `3` `4` `5` `6` `7` `8` `9` `10` `•`   Time Outs: □ 60 sec. `1` `2` `3`
□
□   2nd half `1` `2` `3` `4` `5` `6` `7` `8` `9` `10` `•`   □   30 sec. `1` `2`
                                    1 + 1   2 shots

No.	U	Player	Fouls					SCORING: 3 = 3 point goal 2 = 2 point goal ● = FT made ○ = FT missed			
								1st	2nd	3rd	4th
			1	2	3	4	5				
			1	2	3	4	5				
			1	2	3	4	5				
			1	2	3	4	5				
			1	2	3	4	5				
			1	2	3	4	5				
			1	2	3	4	5				
			1	2	3	4	5				
			1	2	3	4	5				
			1	2	3	4	5				
			1	2	3	4	5				
			1	2	3	4	5				
		_____	Quarter Totals								

Chapter Sixteen

Mapping Out
Sportscasting Territory

Assuming that you can walk in and perform sportscasting without doing any leg work is rather naïve. Sure, you may have a radio station that wants to hire you, a sponsorship deal which rivals the NBA, but don't expect that your venue will be taken care of. People need to know who you are, what you are doing, and above all, go through the approval stages. This is especially true of high schools and colleges, where people cannot simply want onto campus and do whatever they wish.

Credibility – If you have contacts within a high school or college, it goes a long way toward getting your foot in the door. Several times, the first question posed to you will be *"why do you want to do this for us?"* If you reply that *"its for the money,"* you won't see the pavement as it hits you. The last thing you want to do is find a school which already has a broadcaster. Typically, that broadcaster's credibility has been built through years of operation with the school and you shouldn't expect that you can just walk through the door, say *"I've arrived"* and have everything fall into place. Credibility takes work, it takes contacts, and above all, it takes decency.

Dress Attire – Anyone you meet connected with the school needs to respect you. The first way to do this is to show up in business attire. Regardless of how you feel about it, the school needs to determine your credibility. You must play the part if you are going to act in the play. Looking like a slob or someone who doesn't care will have people shrug you off or not return anymore phone calls.

Who To Contact First – When getting your foot in the door, don't wedge it in the wrong doorway, otherwise it may cut off your foot and leave you out in the cold. If you are attempting to broadcast for a high school or college, set up a meeting with the athletic director. Don't involve the basketball coach at this point. Instead, find out what the athletic director wants or thinks. They are the decision maker, not the coach (although a coach may believe otherwise).

The same is true for minor league teams. There are several in which the owner is the general manager and coach, so it various. However, attempting to contact anyone but the top person will likely get you no where. Sports information directors (SIDs) are also a key source to finding the right door to knock on at a college athletic department. You can look up who the sports information director is for a college in your town on the school's athletic website.

Be careful with SIDs though. A lot of them are typically interested in doing only Live Stats as a service for their parents & fans and not sportscasting. Live Stats is a program accessible through websites which shows the statistics as they happen with a 3-5 second delay. While some might find it interesting, most find it extremely boring.

Plan Out What You Are Providing – Are you buying time? Do you have a radio station willing to hire you and provide time for the game? Are you providing web streaming? Are you going to travel to each game or only do home games? You should know these things, any costs which are associated with them, and how you intend to have these services paid for.

Travel Concerns – Smaller colleges and some universities cannot afford to pay for travel expenses of sportscasters. Therefore, this may limit your involvement with that type of school unless you have funding via a radio station or sponsorship, etc. Assuming that you are traveling with the team, without making arrangements for funding or reimbursement, can get you in a ton of hot water.

Sponsorship Concerns – Some colleges and universities may want your product, however, they may not want to align themselves with specific sponsors. In this case, have a set form of guidelines in order to show how you will attain sponsorships etc. For instance, do not expect most schools to align themselves with adult stores, casinos, hard liquor ads or credit card companies. Most schools consider these to be the antithesis of their institution's mission. Be aware of what the school's mission is and be ready to align yourself with it, since you are hoping that the school will align itself with you.

For most minor league teams, that type of stuff goes out the window. Minor league teams may ask for a cut of your sponsorship deal as a matter of a rights fee. Sorry, but you are using their product to sell something. There is a give and a take with everything. However, if you are paying a rights fee, they should be paying for travel to and from their away games.

When to Approach - The best time to approach is 1-2 months after the last season culminated, not 1-2 weeks prior to the season starting. If you wait until the last minute, it is a scramble and likely you will not be the sportscaster for that team. Also, it gives everyone time to digest your proposal, what you intend to do for them, and how you will be compensated.

When Approaching Radio Stations – If you would like to cut to the chase and simply sportscast whatever basketball games a radio station provides, there are two ways to do it. First is to build yourself a killer aircheck. Second, is to hand-deliver a copy of the aircheck and your resume to the radio station's program director.

Making A Killer Resume – Highlight your skills as a sales person. Program directors are busy or just like to act busy. However, if you approach them with the mindset that you will help them sell something, program directors will listen. Program directors are usually fired based on sales at smaller stations, therefore anything that you can help a program director sell is worth about 10 points of interest on your side. People in radio make room for sales people. Air talent is a dime a dozen.

Commercial Call Letters On A Resume - A person with commercial call letters (example: KWUI 94.5 FM) looks great on a resume. Even if you have to work part-time as an announcer, these commercial caller letters get your foot in the door and on your way to a sportscasting career. If you don't have commercial call letters, as long as you have been calling games for a while, there is still hope to get a job, it just way take you promising to sell for the station.

Territory – Don't walk in on someone else's turf and expect to be welcomed with open arms. It can also happen later down the road to you. It is also unprofessional to sell a product, say a boy's high school basketball game, if the school hasn't authorized you to do so in advance. You can't just show up and expect to call a game, you should make all of the right contacts first, ensure that there is no one else you will be infringing on (another sportscaster who has been calling that team's games for 20 years). The general rule is that you respect others, they will respect you.

Planning Ahead – You should always plan a broadcast ahead. This means calling the school where you will be sportscasting that they have internet or phone line, a proper power supply, and to ensure that any other issues can be resolved. You do not want to attempt to resolve these issues at game time. Also, you shouldn't rely on a part-time school staff member at your high school to give you all of the proper details on internet or phone line access.

What you should expect from the school or team:

1. Access (interviews, stats, etc will be provided to you).

2. Professionalism (space at the game table, etc).

3. Potential Sponsorship Opportunities (if they have any sponsorship opportunities available for your broadcast, that they will likely give you the contact information to follow up with that potential sponsor).

THE SPORTSCASTER'S NOTEBOOK

What the school or team should expect from you:

1. Access (broadcast, fairness, & little controversy).

2. Professionalism (treating their players and coaches with respect, especially if they are younger).

Making a Killer Aircheck

Although airchecks for sportscasting are a bit tough, if you fashion your aircheck correctly, you will have success.

Step One: Put about 2 minutes of opening highlights which set up entire plays (don't just include the dunks, but about three plays which set up the action with a culminating finish). Don't put music or anything underneath of the clips because it distracts from what the program director wants to listen to anyway.

Step Two: Place a quarter or half of one basketball game, unedited and continuous, in order to showcase your ability to keep up the action, present a mental picture for the audience through your verbal cues, etc. You had better not be screaming your way through, using a ton of crap lingo and catch phrases. This is where you establish your ability as a sportscaster, not where you make an ESPN highlight.

Step Three: Provide a pregame show to one of your broadcasts (minus the advertisements) which sets up your interviews skills and your intro/opening script.

Chapter Seventeen

Selling Broadcast Sponsorships

Selling Sponsorships

Sportscasters are sales people, whether they like to recognize that or not. Selling sponsorships is the name of the game. It can be a pain in the butt. Especially if you try to prove everyone "wrong" by "going it alone" without any type of help. That is just asking for trouble and misery the closer you get to the sports season without any sales. The first rule of sales: People buy from their friends, or at the very least, people that they like. This is an important thing to recognize. If you choose to sell sponsorships, which you may have to do whether you are working at a radio station, or have an independent podcast or livestream, you face to come to terms with the reality that you are in sales. There are a few things to remember as well.

Face it, sportscasting means sales: You are a sales person. Forget the notion that you are the talent who can turn down the hard work of selling someone on buying ads for your sportscast. That will not happen. And if it does, everyone else in the world would be surprised. You are in sales. This is a business. Either learn to love sales or leave the sportscasting behind. No one will do the job for you. This is something that you have to do to succeed at sports broadcasting. There are no shortcuts.

Set A Sponsorship Cycle In Motion & Stick With It

You should buy a large paper calendar and have a sponsorship sales cycle of at least 200 days prior to the first game of the season. This will allow you enough time to deal with all of the little things that pop up – in-decision, family issues, sponsorship follow-ups, new sales calls, and new prospect leads. You need to join your area's Chamber of Commerce and civic functions such as Rotary International Clubs, where business owners meet. You need to be the face of the game that they hear, become that guy that they want to affiliate with, and sponsor.

You are in sales. Start selling.

Business Cards

You should have business cards with all of your contact information ready to go. Hand them out to anyone who has a business or is near the decision-maker for a business. Make your cards memorable. Find a way for people to keep it, but also remember you specifically, so that they pass it along. Get business cards from every person that you meet, and keep an organized list of your contacts – when you met them, where you met them, etc. Then call them up the following week, setting appointments for coffee or lunch. This is the best way to ensure a quality sale of your sportscast to the general businesses in the area. Most won't care to hear your actual play-by-play. What they want is an honest, fair approach that will get them in front of the right amount of listeners/viewers to bring folks back through their doors. Can you do that? It's all in how you sell it.

Business License & Tax ID

If you are going to be serious about sportscasting as your own business, you are going to have to understand that the government wants a piece of it. Usually, the fee is about $50 for a home-based business, and a EIN Tax ID from the IRS is free, just log onto their website and file. This will also help you legitimize your sportscasting business. When businesses do sponsorship, they do so by invoice and send checks not cash. You will need be ready for when they ask you for your business license (Universal Business Identifier – UBI) and your Tax EIN. This is for their records, so they can write this off as a marketing expense.

The Business Of Sportscasting Is Fun To Talk About

Face it, if you approach someone and tell them that you are in sportscasting, there is at least a mild, if not higher interest in what you do for a career. It's not like insurance or something boring. Working with sports is one of the best foots in the door that you can have with any business. Just about everyone either knows or thinks they know something about sports. And the majority love to talk about it. This is your best way to communicate that you have sponsorship available for local sportscasts. Better yet, you might also be able to help them with tickets to an upcoming game as a sponsor too. Some of the people that you will speak with may not have sponsorship dollars, but the excitement of what you are doing will usually attract others who do. Be patient, keep your eye on the prize and keep active in your approach.

The Secret of Selling Is Who Says What

If you say something good about yourself to a client, it sounds like your ego is talking. If someone else says a great thing about you to a client, consider it money. Part of the secret of selling is to get referrals, people who speak on your behalf. It eliminates the cold calling tactics that garner you people who don't care to talk to you. People don't buy from cold calls, they buy from referrals.

Be Prepared, Look Professional, Be On Time

This is a straight-laced business mentality. Either you understand that people judge on your appearance or you won't. They do not care if you sound like play-by-play gold if you have a pony tail, wear stained sweat pants or show up late to a meeting. Your looks depend on their trust. If you burn a business contact at a meeting and do not show up on time, it will get around to the business community. If you intend to "wing it" then expect to go home without a sale. Sponsorship sales are hard work. They require hard workers who follow through. What you do in the board room says volumes about what you will present at your sportscast.

Be Great On The Phone

You are in the verbal communication field. If you decide not to "give good phone" when you talk to a business prospect, then you better work at it or get out of sportscasting altogether. You need to be able to communicate with people. If you mumble or cannot enunciate, that needs to be corrected immediately. Work on it. Your pitch is your delivery is your sportscast. This means being concise and direct as to what you want from the person on the other end of the phone. Remember, sponsors are busy too.

Set at least 10 appointments each week on Thursday and Friday: The front end of your week should be scheduled appointments for sponsorships. Typically, a Monday through Wednesday schedule is going to get you closer to talking with the decision maker. Use Thursday and Friday appointments to call on sponsors and make follow-ups for the next week. This is a job at this point. Ensure that you have a one-to-two hour window in between each sales call. Mainly because you do not want to be late for another appointment while your first appointment decides to have you re-introduce your sportscast and sponsorship package to one of the other decision-makers in the building.

Find A Decision-Maker

Everyone else in a company who you meet will be someone who cannot make a decision without a person above them approving it. Usually they will end up attempting to road block you from getting anywhere as a gate keeper to the boss. Ask who handles broadcast sponsorship for your inquiry. If you speak to an administrative assistant, ask him/her if they can help you locate that person. When you find the person in charge of sponsorship for the business, feel them out by setting an appointment. If, at the appointment, the person appears not to be the decision maker, help them progress the process into the next step. Ask if you need to attend any meetings with their boss in order to help explain what you are providing to the business in terms of sportscasting sponsorship. Be helpful, not pushy.

People Buy From Their Friends

Learn how to network in business circles. Make more friends than you know what to do with. If you like sitting at home, mindlessly playing video games or are an insular person, than sportscasting is not for you. Everything about this business is sales. It is about meeting people, engaging them, and getting to listen to your presentation about the game on the field or court. Talk to people who know people. Chat up people who will benefit from your sportscast being on the air. Parents of players, boosters, local fans, etc. is a great way to start. Usually they own a business or know someone who does, and can help refer you to them. When they start helping you discover who to speak with, you've got your foot in the door. The line of demarcation is when a friend or colleague recommends you, because it allows those decision-makers justification to providing you extra time to give a sponsorship pitch. Commonly, those people who make the meeting with you, are ready to listen to your pitch, have already made up their mind to do something with you. It is just up to you to put their mind at ease that their decision is the right one. That sponsoring your sportscast is the best value for their advertising dollar.

The Best Inventory Is Limited

It does not matter if it is the first day of your sponsorship selling career. It does not matter if you have 3 million advertising slots to sell. The best inventory that you have is always limited. It is not infinite, it is finite. While you should never openly lie about what you are selling and to whom you are selling to, you should be willing to say that your best inventory is in short supply. Because it is. The best sponsorship slots are not the same as the rest of the sponsorship slots. That means the halftime or second half of the game, when listeners tune in the most to hear the closing action of the game, is limited and determined as the best slots for your customers. And its limited. This language matters. You want your customers to be assured that when they are paying more, there is a reason why.

You should also be willing to share that you have other appointments with other prospective sponsors, who may always want those short supply slots for their sponsorship as well. If your prospective sponsor asks who your sponsors are, have a good answer. Also ensure that you are meeting with sponsors and their competitors within the same week. It makes certain that they know that when you are talking to one car dealership, you are talking to them all, and it builds up a competition to be the main sponsor for that industry. That includes exclusivity deals, which means that you should be charging more – 200-percent more – than normal rates with a longer-term contract in place, which keeps you from going after sponsorship from that competitor.

Always Get The Money Up-Front, The Contract Signed

Handshake deals are worth what is written down on paper. Ray Kroc did a handshake deal for 1 percent of McDonald's annual profits to the McDonald's brothers when they sold him the company – 1 percent is worth $100 million annually in 2022 dollars – the McDonald's brothers saw nothing of that handshake deal. That's because handshake deals have little to no proof in terms of the carry-out of the contract. Get your sponsorship deal in writing via a contract.

Go to a lawyer, pay for their services and get a template in MS Word that you can use several times over, but do not rely on some computer program or blanket legalize service if you want to have that contract binding. Contracts have to be written in a state or recognized by a state if written in another state, in order to be binding. A lot of them aren't. Which is why you need a lawyer, in the state that you are residing in, to ensure that a sponsorship contract is valid not void. If a sponsor acts edgy about a contract, that means that they will want to back out at any point if they don't see an immediate return. That should be a red flag that they aren't serious.

Be Friendly With Tire Kickers

Expect to have several hundred meetings with potential sponsors prior to going into the season. Expect more than a few to have several meetings that literally go nowhere. These prospects are "tire kickers" and tend to feel people out. They are people who don't know want to know you. They are unsure of your product. And they tend to want to keep knowing that you are serious about what you are doing before they decide to commit, which they likely won't. It is part of the process.

Trade Does Not Pay The Bills

Do not take trade. It will not help you land an advertiser who will pay money later on. It is better not to deal with someone who wants to provide you with trade. They tend to tell other potential sponsors that they got a trade deal, and all that does is reduce your product's value. Plus, the trade is always less than what cash would have been in the deal.

THE SPORTSCASTER'S NOTEBOOK

Rate Formula

Figure out the cost of time for each advertisement run, divided by the total ad time per hour, plus 100 percent. You have a finite inventory of good time slots available. So use them.

Three Different Price Points

People love deals. They also love different tastes. Some just want to dip their toe into the sponsorship. Some want to have the maximum amount possible of sponsorship so they can blanket advertise your broadcast. You need to have three different price points available to help each sponsor find exactly the right fit for their dollar.

Setting Pricing

Set a maximum price, at least 150-250 percent higher than your lower price, and offer sponsorship spots on your broadcast for it. The middle price should be 75-95 percent higher than your lower price, but not give much more air time than your lowest price offers. With the lowest price, offer a bargain basement price which is about 50 percent above your total costs to provide the sportscast. Also have a method of bumping smaller sponsorships into bigger ones. You want to sell as many medium sponsorships as possible.

Why Selling More Medium Sponsorships Is Good

You need your inventory filled. You need it filled prior to your first sportscast. It creates demand and allows you to tell your prospects that your current sponsorships are stacked, and unless they intend to purchase at a higher sponsorship rate than you currently have, they will have to wait until next year, when the prices might be higher, but inventory might be available. Prospects love to keep up with the Jones, especially if they are getting shut out of a good deal.

You Need To Do Follow-up To Earn The Sale

Sales rarely happen on the first call. People need time to think. To ensure that they are making the right decision. Be patient. You need to continue to follow up every few weeks to earn that sale.

Face-To-Face Is Just As Important

Meeting someone face-to-face is 10 times more effective than just a random call on the phone. Anyone can call on the phone. It means something to people when you meet with them, selling them through trust. It also allows people to have their questions answered and develop a good strategy for whether or not they should be supporting and sponsoring your sportscast.

Attend As Many Organized Functions As You Can

People love to talk sports. So you will instantly be a hit and have your opportunity. Attend every chamber luncheon or civic group function as you can when meeting people. Do not sit in the corner with your friends. Hand out as many business cards as possible. Exchange business cards with others. Get to know the people who are around you. Know them. Become their friend. Sell them quicker. It is the process of understanding that humans require trust to create commerce with each other.

Do not simply "sell" people at meetings by vomiting out a giant sales pitch. This rings as false and is usually the best possible way to lose a sale. There are several business-to-business meetings in every city, but no one wants to speak to an insurance salesman (usually reminds people of their own mortality).

Sports on the other hand is an instant connector. You can speak about an upcoming game schedule, or the current or past year, or a player or coach who is a genius for the team. Everything you say is more likely to sell if you keep it positive, exciting and about how the potential sponsor can be part of the action.

Don't Get Lazy Because of New Technology

You need to pound the pavement. That means physical meetings with potential clients. E-mails get erased. They are easy to ignore. Especially if they are send unsolicited. You need to have face-to-face interactions, so the decision-maker can trust you with their brand and their money. Don't be an e-mail spam king. It's usually annoying and wins zero sales.

Retention Is Because of Value Received (It's A 2-Way Street)

If you sell a business on sponsoring your sportscast, you need to make extra sure that they are receiving value in return. That means that you hand out extra flyers to fans in the venues that you sportscast their games in. That means telling the football team to eat at the restaurant once a week. Sponsorship means that they are taking a big risk, a large chance, on your sportscast bringing them business. Most companies are not Pepsi or Walmart and worried about branding. They are worried about driving actual awareness and business through their doors.

These companies need to track that their sponsorship with your sportscast is effective and brings people to spend money with them. They cannot afford blanket advertising to not direct gain for themselves. If a small business spends money with you, it had better translate into a return on investment for them. Not only can you harm a business owner by not giving them return value, but you also potentially cost other businesses from receiving sponsorship as well. That is not a good thing. Karma is a bad business killer.

If You Attempt To "Close" Someone On A Sales Too Quick, You Lose Their Interest

People are jaded. They know when they are being "closed" on a sales pitch. The limited time offer does not make anyone feel urgent about buying a sponsorship. In fact, it may be considered a turn-off. You should be willing to continue answering their questions, attempting to help them through the entire process toward a bigger decision of buying sponsorship with you.

Added Value Principle

The more added value, beyond what a sponsor had already expected to receive for what their dollar, the more likely they will return as a sponsor for the following broadcast or season. One method sportscasters have in their toolkit is to get a banner from the sponsor, and have it placed up in the gym with the permission of the team. Or hand out flyers, bumper stickers, from that sponsor. This costs you nothing, but the sponsor sees what you are doing and appreciates it.

Listenership

Any sponsor is going to attempt to discover what your listenership is for your sportscasts. It is important to them that you aren't broadcasting into a sea of white noise. The great thing about the Internet is that there are actual numbers, with duration clicks of how long they listened to the presentation and when. It is a good idea to showcase how long someone devotes to listening to your broadcast. A great way to illustrate this is through an average time equation concept. Define what the difference is in average time that a person in your area listens to any broadcast, and the average time that a person in your area listens to your sportscast. If you are purchasing blocks of airtime from a local radio station or are working for one, the demographic information for their listenership on their own advertising packages should be available.

Income of Listenership

Put yourself in the mindset of your sponsor. Find the information that they would want to know if you were considering sponsoring an item. Remember, as a sponsor, you want to see people returning back through your doors. Nothing is done for charity and your investment in any advertisement would need to show a return. As a business owner, you would also want to ensure that you are targeting the right people with your sponsorship dollars. You may want to target females (ages 34-54) or residents with earning higher income than $45,000 per year. A car dealer does not want to target children (ages 10-17) who do not make $45,000 a year. They want their parents to be listening who are in that demographic. You have to define who is listening and what demographics they serve.

All of this depends on what your listenership is. Who do you believe that as a sportscaster, you are trying to reach? The internet streaming numbers will break it down, and it may surprise you. It also may surprise the businesses who see your numbers and demographics as well. Gaining sponsorship from a business which does not hit your target audience's interests does little good for anyone. Break down average times that your listeners' age and income demographics are listened. This will help the potential sponsor on why they should invest.

Price Levels & Value of Sponsorship: There needed to be several packaged levels of sponsorship for specific events. As shown below:

1 Headline Sponsorship of "Coaches Show" $5,000
1 Headline Sponsorship of "Pregame Show" $2,500
1 Headline Sponsorship of "Postgame Show" $1,500
"Dunk of the Night" Sponsorship - $750
"Touchdown of the Night" Sponsorship - $750

Such as a dunk mention or a touchdown. These are wrapped into the overall package selection, to help entice that you will give a bit extra to the sponsor. Notice that these types of package/quad-level pricing are already deceptive compared to the rules of what we set up in the chapter earlier. Why? Because it allows the sponsor to see how much it costs to "own" the broadcast as well as leaving some flexibility for the sportscaster to create new inventory.

The real pricing is $2,500 to $1,500 to $1,000. This structure is setup to allow the sponsor to feel as if they can reach the secondary top level ($2,500) without it being the highest paid amount of the broadcast. Many sponsors will go for the top level rather than the second or mid-level simply because they want to "own" the sportscast.

Chapter Eighteen

Understanding The
Sports Information Director (SID)

While Chapter 20 is dedicated lin this book to overall ways to build solid relationships in your sportscasting career, I felt it was worth it to cover a larger relationship that you should really work on. This relationship goes beyond everything else in the sportscasting world and with you as a sportscaster: **the relationship between you and the sports information director / team communications officer (SID)**. This is a main press conduit for your access to everything running smoothly within the high school or collegiate athletic department or team. You can create a huge issue for yourself by not recognizing this fact.

Athletic directors and coaches tend to promise the moon. They also believe that they are in charge of things. And they are... except for the details. That's where a SID comes into play. While an athletic director can make some initial waves to allow you approval, it is really the detail that is beset on other entities. And anything that concerns the press means that it falls under the domain of the SID. The SID runs the overall show, even if it doesn't seem like it. I had a friend who told me that anytime he had a sales pitch to a company where he was meeting with an executive, he always made friends with the administrative assistant whose desk was right outside the executive's door. Because that administrative assistant has more power than you think. They can sabotage a deal or ensure that you never gain another appointment, all on how you treat them, using the power that they wield but usually don't let you know that they have it. An SID operates in similar fashion.

SIDs can make or break your experience as a sportscaster. The entire night of game space, as well as advanced information, can be directed by how SIDs view you as well as your operation. Sure, the coach or athletic director may return a text, but that's only if they want to reveal something to you. SIDs on the other hand, know everything going on within the athletic department or team. They also have all of the statistics, not just current but historical as well as player comparable, that a coach or athletic director won't have. And SIDs tend to control the physical space of the game table / booth seating assignments, including where all of the electrical outlets are, the WiFi passwords, press passes, and access to the locked, clean private bathroom. No, I'm not kidding. If there's something that you need access to, including scheduling with a coach or athletic director for a press interview, you need to go through the SID. They are the controller of all of that access. And much like the administrative assistant sitting at a desk outside of an executive's office, they have more power than you might perceive.

Most, if not all SIDs, are going to be thrilled if you present the option of doing a play-by-play sportscast at their facility if they do not have one currently. Since 2008 when **The Sportscaster's Notebook** was first published, the media landscape has changed. It has also broadened the ability for more sportscasting, not less, to be put out through digital means. Usually, women's sports were given limited access due to inclusion barriers. No longer can there be a claim that there is only so much space on the radio station dial for games, which usually meant that women's sports were shut out in favor of men's sports. With audio and video livestreaming capabilities, every sport has a shot to be on the air, along with the need for sportscasters to conduct play-by-play. There are always more options out there, if you as a sportscaster aren't limiting yourself to solely attempting to do the men's sports, specifically football, basketball or baseball. And SIDs are welcoming to new sportscasting avenues that increase the media attention for their other sports. That's their job. As long as you aren't a jerk and follow the SID's lead on certain things.

SIDs will require a few things from you as a sportscaster – first is to be a good citizen toward your fellow press mates and the team, and the second is to be on-time. They do not want anyone entering the gym, game table or booth brazenly walking onto their turf, attempting to usurp their area of command. It's not only downright disrespectful, but also a way to look for trouble. If you want to see how SIDs can help a sportscaster's success on the air, look at the sportscaster who is being nice, pleasant and thankful for whatever they are given. SIDs tend to gravitate toward those who are accommodating to them given the high-stress environment that SIDs are in.

Sportscasters need to work hard at their own tasks such as calling the game, but who also ask for anything needed as far in advance as possible. Not five minutes prior to or after tip-off. If you wanted it badly enough, you should have looked at the assignment / rundown sheet provided by the SID, including the badly needed WiFi codes. Don't wait until after the action has started to request things. That includes your power supply needs, such as electrical plug-ins, which should be planned out with the SID in advance. Simply showing up with a bunch of equipment, without clearing your presence with the SID, is really silly and, again, looking for trouble. SIDs are not your servants. Nor are they beneath you. While there is some stature to being a sportscaster, you should remember that SIDs are full-time staff at most universities and half-time staff at high schools. They deserve your respect for their position as well as time accommodating your requests.

This level of respect also includes not going around the SID for permissions by asking the athletic director or head coach for things. Sure, the coach will agree to everything that you ask for, but won't follow through with any of it. Mainly because the coach has to run a team on the court / field, and there's an SID to deal with those press requests. The coach isn't going to worry about the hot dog prices at the concession stand either. So don't expect the coach to concern themselves with where a sportscaster's seat is being assigned. If there are legitimate issues with the seat assignments for a sportscaster, such as a blocking issue where the play-by-play announcer cannot concentrate because someone seated next to them is noisy, then the SID can handle that seat assignment request and move you. This is what the SID, not the coach, is tasked with doing. Remember that the SID has a role here.

SIDs are typically at their busiest after Wednesday afternoons for the rest of the week, stretching sometimes into Sunday nights. That means that your window for requests should be Monday or Tuesday when you can reach out, chat with them, or even take them to lunch (which you should buy). This helps get the SID on board with what you are doing, and lets them know that you respect their authority within the media request process. SIDs are happy to arrange interviews with players and coaches for your halftime shows in advance, or communicate with you on issues at game's end so that a live interview can take place before your show ends. But the more that you request things last minute from SIDs, the less likely that you will receive those requested items. Because SIDs get asked for all kinds of stuff. If you saw their e-mail inbox, you'd shudder but also understand.

This is especially true of collegiate SIDs. They have to handle 20-30 sports, sometimes without an assistant director. Sometimes they have some student workers helping them. SIDs are dealing with a lot of different coaching and player needs coming at them, from multiple sports, in every direction. What they expect from a play-by-play announcer is that all of the sportscaster's needs will be addressed far in advance, meaning days or weeks, when it comes to the mundane stuff like seating assignments. At the very least, sportscasters can go a long way by being nice and realizing that SIDs want you to be successful too. SIDs now have to handle an assortment of things that weren't that relevant in 2008, including bloggers/tweeters/podcasters who feel that they should just be as relevant in press credentials as a print, television, or radio journalist. And those digital journalists may have a point, since the amount of traffic coming from their website dwarfs most of the metrics from traditional journalism. All of this comes down to the consideration that the SID is there to help you. They have a lot on their plate and need your patience in achieving your mutual goal: Getting a quality broadcast live for their games.

A big factor in this is how you decide to conduct yourself as a sportscaster and as a professional. While you are the play-by-play guy for the home team, it is kind of dumb to also try and cheer or make noise or be somehow obstructive in a homerish way when the mic isn't "hot." Do whatever you want when the mic is "hot" that livens up the broadcast. But when the mic is "cold," you need to act like a professional. Don't heckle the opposing players or coach. Don't try to hide anything that the opposition needs or block them out of asking for something. If you do, the SID will hear about it from the opposition, and you will have to be dealt with. Everyone, including yourself, should act like a professional and hold yourself up to a standard of decorum that is representative of the team or school that you are broadcasting for. This also comes down to the way that you handle the rest of the game table / booth staff. Some of these folks have been volunteers for decades, and they should be treated as well as provide the same respect that you provide them. In some ways, they've witnessed every type of game for that team, so they may have more institutional knowledge than you do about the team you are providing play-by-play for.

SIDs are a conduit toward more statistics and other information than any other place you will have access to. They can help you with gaining stories or other tidbits which can grow your overall sportscast. If you attempt to sideline or circumvent them, do so at your own peril: An SID rarely forgets when they get burned by a journalist or member of the press. One time, I recall a press member going to the athletic director for a "private conversation," complaining about the SID, then having the SID called into the athletic directors' office while the press member was still there, to be chewed out. Needless to say, while the press member won that small exchange, they lost a bigger one, because the SID never really trusted them again. This is what happens when you burn someone by going around their authority. You make more enemies than you don't need than friends.

SIDs should be presented with a large measure of respect by sportscasters for the thankless, daily job that they do. There is a lot more happening with SIDs than simply game night duties. This is why you should look at taking SIDs out to lunch as well as picking up the tab every once in a while. You want certain people in the athletic department or team to be on your side. Especially someone such as an SID, who is communicating with their fellow SIDs at other athletic departments or teams, on a daily basis. There are plenty of potential opportunities for better sportscasting jobs out there, but it all depends on the current SID that you are working with. Did you treat that SID well? Are they going to provide you a valuable reference when better sportscasting jobs come available? Remember, talent is a far lower component in sportscasting than reliability and likeability. It all depends on how you treat others. Especially the SID.

Chapter Nineteen

Hockey
&
Volleyball
Play-By-Play

HOCKEY SPORTSCASTING

Hockey is a sport of continuous action which holds the same principles as basketball and volleyball when describing speed as a part of the game flow. Hockey however crosses over both basketball and volleyball, using both location of players and the puck on the ice, as well as description of how the puck is passed, intercepted or shot.

Notice the two diagrams on the next page for hockey, which showcase both the net and what may occur on the ice which details the various spots where the action may be happening. This is used in reference point to each play, after the play has either culminated or been isolated to one specific area. This mirrors the principle of basketball sportscasting, which presents a mental picture through the action's location on the playing surface.

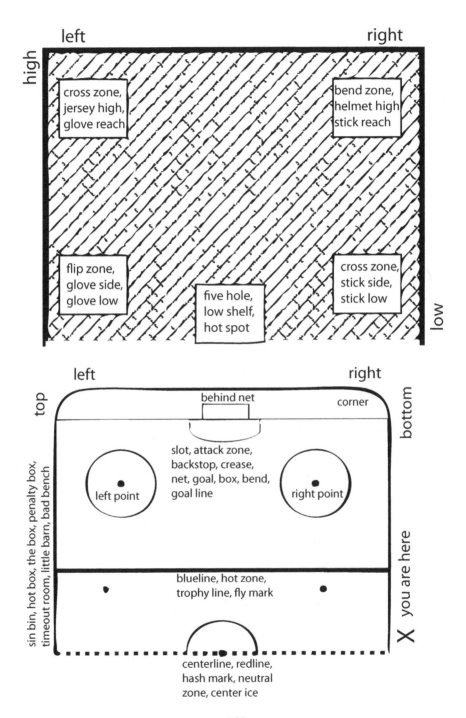

left   right

high

cross zone,
jersey high,
glove reach

bend zone,
helmet high
stick reach

flip zone,
glove side,
glove low

five hole,
low shelf,
hot spot

cross zone,
stick side,
stick low

low

left   right

top   bottom

behind net   corner

slot, attack zone,
backstop, crease,
net, goal, box, bend,
goal line

left point   right point

sin bin, hot box, the box, penalty box,
timeout room, little barn, bad bench

blueline, hot zone,
trophy line, fly mark

X you are here

centerline, redline,
hash mark, neutral
zone, center ice

THE SPORTSCASTER'S NOTEBOOK

VOLLEYBALL SPORTSCASTING

Sportscasting for volleyball matches is intense and different that even those fast-paced games such as hockey or basketball. The intensity comes from quick-rotations, hammering swings, and the score rapidly changing via a point being awarded every time. In order to offer the best audio broadcast possible for volleyball, you must be intent on knowing the game itself calling the motion of the ball, the player names, and keep up with the action.

Example: Titans versus Rainbows

The Titans Beau served the ball into play and the description of the serve was called. The ball went over the net to Arron, who received it and hit it up for Wae to serve. Wae's serve was attacked by Stephens who hit the ball back over the net into Titans defense, hitting off of the Titan's blockers and scored a point for Rainbows.

Example play call: *"Titans Beau sends across a jump floater to Arron, to Wae, for Stephens plays a heavy swing off the block for the point, 1-0 Rainbows."*

The principle of this basic volleyball play calling is to determine who serves the ball, who receives it, and how does the play continue or end. It is not necessary to always call a dig, a set upon reception, or the attack. These are common enough that if they do not add to the broadcast, they stretch the amount of description you give during the play, thus you may miss something as volleyball's speed really kicks up with every point.

During every reset, when there is a timeout on the court, you should always come back with a mention of the rotation for each side, naming off each of the players and which position they are in.

The clock itself is unimportant, however the score is. Name the score after each point and only the match score when the game score is nearing match point.

Where the ball lands is not as important as how the ball was played. However, if you feel you can describe this information post-play, it will add to the value of the listeners' mental picture.

There are several different ways to describe the motion of the ball which will help you break down and isolate each player's actions if necessary.

Ball Crossing The Net Descriptions
"Sends it across" – *"Brings it back"* – *"Floater"* – *"Pushes it back over"* – *"Stays alive over the net"* – *"Joust over the net"* – *"Clears the net"*

Ball Being Received From Attack or Serve
"Keeps it up" – *"Brings it back"* – *"Going for the push"* – *"Sends it up"* – *"Roll shot"* – *"Handled by"* – *"Plays it off the line"*

Ball Being Defended From Attack or Serve
"Off the block" – *"Misses the block"* – *"Passed back to"* – *"Backrow to"* – *"Off the scramble"* – *"Backrow for ball"* – *"Dives to keep it alive"* – *"Second timer"*- *"Backrow ball"* – *"Blocked but keeps it over"*

Ball Being Set For An Attack
"Going to set it up" – *"Rolls it over"* – *"Quiet off the set"* – *"Tosses a floater"* – *"Sets up for"* – *"Goes to the outside"* – *"Shoots a backhander"*

THE SPORTSCASTER'S NOTEBOOK

Ball Being Attacked

"Gets a swing" – "Gets another crack at it" – "Hits slide right" – "Leaps and kills it" – "Pumps and jumps" – "Hits it low" - "Going for the swing" – "Unloads another" – "Has a heavy swing" – "Comes out of the back row to hit"

Ball Attacked Successfully

"Off the hands" – "Out of bounds" – "Hits the tape" – "Wipes off the block" – "Ball goes long" - Can't handle it" – "Loses it off the line"

During the play action, the location of where the ball landed will probably be the least of your concerns. The quickness with which a play with happen and interact with the players involved, will give you enough to worry about. However, one of the benefits of sub outs and the stoppage of play after the point prior to the next serve is that you can split up the court and recall the location of where the ball landed.

In the diagram below, one half of a volleyball court is shown. It is split up to illustrate an easy reference system in which every ball landing hits a specific location on the court. This should help as you recall a play, giving a short analysis of each attack and how it was defended.

Example: *"Browning took the serve to the outside right for Keri whose swing landed on the back center of the court in between the block for the point."*

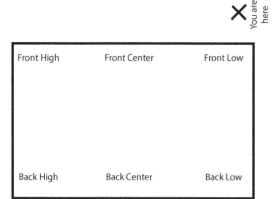

Chapter Twenty

Broadcast Equipment

I had to chuckle when I arrived at the 2008 version of this chapter on broadcast equipment. Those recommendations were of a different time and era, where equipment was harder to procure back before Amazon made it very easy to order anything and get it within a day or a few hours, depending on your residential location. Most of the equipment that I listed in the 2008 version of *The Sportscaster's Notebook* is no longer relevant. It was great equipment for its time, but in 2022 and beyond, it really would hold you back, rather than move you forward. That's because technology changes. Everything is about adapting or dying. Technology enhances its capability, speeds up, corrects hurdles or barriers, and ends up reducing the overall consumer price to obtain the latest product.

There were several issues that I was attempting to overcome when I listed most of that equipment back in the 2008 version of *The Sportscaster's Notebook*. Mainly because in 2008, there were online protocol steps to take in order to access a livestream. That included using encoder software to build up a livestream. Those barriers no longer exist. In order to achieve a successful livestream, encoders aren't a factor or something that those who are sportscasting would likely even know about. Specifically because the majority of new livestreaming websites or properties have enabled a seamless transition from point-to-point, where the broadcaster starts the livestream and it goes to the consumer, without either party knowing that the encoder is already part of the website itself. That's how technology enhances itself, by making it where you don't even recognize the processes that years prior were barriers to entry to access it.

An interesting comparison is when I took the original 2008 Adobe CS1-CS2 files and opened them for access on the Adobe InDesign 22 software platform. The old files didn't like being called up into the new system. It took a while to process because of all the archaic code in CS1-CS2 that was no longer relevant in the Adobe InDesign 22 version. I actually thought that my MacBook Pro was going to crash, simply trying to help open such a heavy-coded past version of the files. Let's just say that by the time it actually opened the 2008 CS1-CS2 files, I was able to make myself a few cups of coffee while the cursor wheel spun various pinwheeled colors for a bit.

This comes back to the physical equipment recommendations that I offered back in 2008. Those are no longer relevant. And in 14 years, if I listed any physical technology in the 2022 version of *The Sportscaster's Notebook*, it would be just as irrelevant as the items that I listed back in 2008. Instead of needing several components in order to develop a credible sportscast, it really comes down to a few in 2022: You'll need a strong computer device, an internet connection, a sound mixer, and a headset with a microphone front. What would have cost you a few thousand dollars in 2008 to purchase could be reasonably obtained in 2022 for less than a few hundred. Everything in technology comes down in price and increases in availability. Back in 2008, laptops were not cheap, WiFi was still being developed, and microphone-fronted headsets were something that you had to back-order and would cost hundreds of dollars. Smart phones were available as infancy version 1 items, which meant that they held about as much data storage as an iPod and not much else.

In 2022 and beyond, a standard cell phone could connect both to the livestream and keep a WiFi connection, as well as plug into a small USB mixer along with an online gamer headset. You could even reduce the need for the USB mixer if you are doing the sportscast solo and can adjust the volume output of your voice to keep it from "scuzzing out" (i.e. being too loud, unlistenable) to the streaming audience. If you do require a laptop rather than using a smart phone, you could get a Chromebook and a portable WiFi device with a monthly carrier charge which would handle the same issues as the phone.

Most of the audio editing software is free and available from the cloud. That means, the only barrier on readiness is you. And that is why this chapter is so easy to write, compared to 2008, when I had to do a lot of research in how to explain accessing an encoder to create a livestream portal. There isn't much in the way of barriers to creating an accessible sportscast livestream anymore. It is truly up to you to build out your own system, then go forward toward the process of creating your own sports broadcast.

Chapter Twenty-One

*Constant Education
of the
Sportscaster*

If there is a consistent message throughout this book, it is one of constant education by the reader/sports broadcaster. You cannot get away with doing the bare minimum that sportscasters did decades ago to survive. The media landscape has changed. The need for sportscasters has also changed with it. Those days of grabbing a hot mic and "winging it" until you find your voice are over. Teams, venues, and listeners expect things done perfectly, going beyond what was needed in the 1970s, where fewer people were critical of a sportscaster's skills. If it got on radio or television back then, people gave it a pass. Now, there are too many options, too many outlets, for those screw-ups to go unnoticed. It follows logically that it is too easy to lose opportunities in sportscasting by "winging it" because you chose not to educate yourself or prepare accordingly.

Either you decide to constantly learn, to hone in on your craft, or you will not make it in this industry. There are too many people who want an opportunity to break into and stay in the field, and the last thing that a broadcaster should ever feel is absolutely comfortable enough that they do not work on their skill set. That is also the message of this book: **Adapt or die.** You make that choice. You must decide that you are going to focus on building up your sportscasting acumen. That you are going to put in the work. This is not different than the players on the field, who practice every day to perfect their craft. Do not let the concept that you've learned enough ever be possible. Always do better. Let your colleagues and local legends decide to "phone in" their sportscasting opportunities by regressing. You need to supercharge your career by continuing to learn. It should be a wake-up call for you, as a sportscaster, when you hear or detect a fellow sportscaster no longer perfecting their game by constantly improving. Chances are, they will be retired out by the team, or downright replaced, because they decided to become dispassionate about the game that they are calling.

As outlined in a previous chapter, the boot camp is a way that shows a constant and consistent education of the sportscaster. Sitting in a spare room or office, door closed to the outside world, hammering out a lot of the calls - that is what makes the sportscaster better. Consider the preparation that you are taking in, ensuring that your broadcast is unique and desirable to listen to. Your prep makes your broadcast better than the rest. Putting in the work matters. It pushes forward the effort and initiative of improving your game, while others are falling behind by doing the bare minimum. Other sportscasters, including those who are working for the opposing team or rival radio/ television stations, aren't putting in the work themselves. They are conditioned to be only as good as they are now, if not worse as their skills regress. It isn't talent alone that gets you the win, it's the hard work before the game is being played that makes you better at your craft.

Consider that you should be honing your sportscasting skills even when you don't get paid to do so. If this is truly the industry that you want to be a part of, you need to work your voice constantly. Not just your vocal cords, but the voice inside of your head. The one that captures everything that your eyes see and your ears hear, then dissects it down into information that you relay back through your mouth into the hot mic. Call out every situation in front of you in a mall. See the spontaneity surrounding you. The downfall of bad sportscasting is that the broadcasters tend to hold back when in public away from the mic. They are quieter or talk casually except when they are doing the play-by-play of a game in front of them. Consider how defeatist this must be to their mind, to see random situations in front of them in the real world and not be able to relay them out by calling that action accordingly.

Those sportscasters are giving up original, one-shot opportunities to witness and call out situations which can improve their skill when doing play-by-play later on the court. By not doing this, they aren't preparing as effectively as they could. This isn't about making a few home run calls either. Or attempting to grab hold of a signature call that you can do over and over again, because that's the way old time sportscasters did their play-by-play. That world has come and gone. This is a new time now. This is about ensuring that you can speak coherently about an in-bounds play off of the baseline, changing up the wording midsentence, creating a great description of an entirely unique opportunity that is comfortable to you.

Another methodology of constant education is whiteboarding up a game. This is where you use a room's whiteboard and a dry erase marker, then draw out the lines, figuring out how to share different types of information. Coaches do it with their players. Sportscasters can do it as well. You can also use your cell phone to time out a shot clock scenario, or just a portion of the game. Give yourself a chance to push the envelope of what type of play that you can call and how you are going to do it. Doing so will allow you to pace yourself, catch your breath, and smooth out your language in an effortless and coherent manner. When you run out of breath, you stop making sense. Imagine how that feels to the radio/television audience hearing you. Notice that the way that you talk pushes or slows the pace of the game, because of the energy that you are using. Are you speeding up the game, or slowing it down, when the opposite is happening with the plays on the court or field? All of it comes down to the sportscaster's tone as the action unfolds.

Whatever you do to increase your constant education as a sportscaster, see it as an investment toward becoming better. Rent is always due for the success that you achieve. The more work you put in, the better you will be compared to those with more "talent" who put in zero or little work whatsoever. You are attempting to bring your audience into a world beyond just the game itself. You are exploring new avenues with your voice, allowing people to understand through your constant learning environment. To paraphrase the poet Emily Dickinson (1830-1886), "Find your nerve. Go beyond it."

Chapter Twenty-Two

Relationship Building

I am not in the position that I am in today without the people who have supported me to this point. There are a few folks who took time out of their work weeks to help me edit and cultivate this book into a 2022 version: **Chris Thompson, Jason Behenna, Wade Fisher, Vance Dawson and Justin Kesterson**. They dropped many things that they were doing in their personal lives in order to help make this 2022 version come to fruition. And they did it because I asked them to. Relationships matter. Every relationship is worth attempting to build into a greater friendship. No exceptions.

These aren't relationships built on the idea of getting money out of them or a job opportunity. These were set relationships where people wanted to help me, because I have helped them. Because they want me to succeed. You need to find those types of relationships for yourself as well. The people that you end up meeting, the conversations that you end up building, they all transform and grow into a larger part of the success that you end up achieving. No one person achieves anything alone. No one wins by isolating themselves. Because all they are doing is isolating themselves from potential opportunities of success.

How you treat people matters. Equity and respect matter. Being nice to the point of overly nice matters. Not being a gossip poison spreader matters. No one wants that type of person in their life. Nor do they want to see that type of person succeed. Everything is about how you treat others and the opportunities that unfold will follow. Your play-by-play skills could be awesome, on point, but your attitude may end up costing you jobs down the road. At the end of the day, its more about whether those hiring you to do play-by-play want you at their Christmas party, than merely the skillset you bring as announcer. Think about that for a moment.

You might find those last two sentences absurd. But think about the way that people engage with others. Think about the way you engage with others. Folks are willing to look past the minor mistakes of people who they like or are nice to them. They are also willing to jump on the mistakes of those who are rude or mean to them. Treat people with respect as if your career might depend on it. Because it probably will.

Chapter
Twenty-Three

Final Thoughts

Below are some final thoughts that were random in nature, but probably needed to be addressed somewhere. Beyond those thoughts, on the final pages, are field/court marks and terms for anyone wishing to sportscast other events such as a volleyball, ice hockey, football, and baseball. With the help of several coaches, just about every term imaginable was written down and included.

Don't Just Shout

Dick Vitale is one thing, you are another, and Brian Bosworth is another. Vitale uses his voice to feed off the energy of the crowd, etc., but it does tend to be a television experience, not an audio one. Vitale also does stop screaming when the energy of the court takes over the energy of the crowd. Brian Bosworth, a former NFL player who served a color analyst for the defunct 2021 XFL, *screamed* every time he opened his mouth. Bosworth's stint with the XFL was termed as "white noise," distracting instead of enhancing the broadcast. Just a thought on different styles.

What Format of Broadcast to Use

Radio Stations typically have various phone receiver boxes which use a POTS line, the best phone line possible. However the receiver does work well with PBX lines. Some of this is greek to the sportscaster, but the radio engineer at the station should be able to answer any questions you have on this. A lot of this lingo was written back for the 2008 book. Is it still as relevant in 2022? Likely not. But it is good to know your broadcast history.

Direct Internet is preferred when going with an audio stream. Wireless Internet dims in and out, meaning your broadcast will sound the same to anyone at home listening. Cellular phone sportscasts sound like crap and should be avoided, especially because all it takes is a cloud in the sky for you to get one bar on your phone and the thing goes dead right as the team makes a come back.

Rundown Sheets

When dealing with a minor league team or college which has an SID, you will typically get a rundown sheet. Request your sheet via email about a day prior, in order to ensure that you are aware of any changes to it. The rundown sheet will detail when the coach or a player that you need to interview for the pregame show is available. It may also help you snag an opposing coach or player if you also want their inclusion into your show.

Voice Levels

If the needle or meter bounces in the red on your sound mixer while you talk, then falls back down, you are alright. If the needle or meter stays in the red and never falls back down, it means you need to lower the volume on your microphone. Otherwise it distorts the sound of your microphone and leaves your sportscast sounding like crap.

Court Microphone

Frankly, a microphone on the court does nothing to enhance the broadcast. Why? Because your headset will usually pick up enough sound off of the floor. Some sportscasters swear by them, use your discretion and try out a few different ways. One size does not fit all.

Media Timeouts

Some high school leagues have media timeouts, other leagues do not. The NCAA and NAIA both adhere to media timeouts and some junior colleges do as well. It all depends on where you are at. Make sure that you have the athletic director or sports information director alert the referees that you have a media broadcast and let them make the call. Media timeouts are a boon for sportscasts, so you should attempt to have them at every game, because you can sell sponsorships at those breaks too.

Sports Information Directors

SIDs are typically stat geeks who can write. I've covered this in Chapter 18. Even they will tell you that and be proud of it. If you need help at the game table, SIDs are the ones who can provide it for you, especially if it is a rule or stats question. Most SIDs adhere to the rules and regulations of CoSIDA, their membership organization.

What that means to you is that most CoSIDA members, if not all, will provide you with one or two game table places (if you bring a stats person), a stats sheet printed out at every timeout, a link to Live Stats (if they have it), a media guide of their team, game notes detailing information about both teams as well as players & coaches before and after the game.

Don't assume anything, especially on the road. It is best to have your school's SID contact the opponent's SID, arrange all of the things you need (internet, phone line, game table space, etc.) prior to arriving. Nothing makes an SID more friendly than a person who shows up unannounced and thinks they run the show. In fact, SIDs will likely prove to you who runs the show at the game table.

Promote Your Broadcast

Regardless of which venue you have your audio broadcast on, you need to promote it. No one will know about it unless you tell them. So make sure that you do. Some ideas include having a friend hand out flyers about the audio broadcast at games, telling the PTA about the broadcasts in order to get them to listen, calling up the sports editor at the local newspaper to make sure that the broadcast is listed along with the game times. Promote, promote, promote. You are doing this not only for yourself but for your sponsors who have invested in you.

Extra Things to Bring

Include a long orange extension cord, a power strip, extra batteries for the laptop and sound mixer, and anything else you can think of. Every place is different and don't expect everyone to have everything, if you call up two days before and ask. Assume the worst and pray for the best.

THE SPORTSCASTER'S NOTEBOOK

On Their Time

When setting up interviews, remember that while time is money for you, the coaches and players also have other outside interests that absorb their time. That being said, don't get frustrated with lateness out of the coaches and players you are attempting to interview, they are doing you a favor. While this may be something you want to disagree with, until you let them in on your profit sharing, don't expect them to be totally eager to show up instantly upon command.

Different Voices

Newspaper don't refuse ink and radio loves different voices. When developing any type of commercials or intros to the pregame, game and postgame, use different voices to narrate. Find your spouse or a little kid (this actually works wonders because people like to listen to little kids). Different voices makes your broadcast sound more professional, as if you have a team of people surrounding you, and enlivens the broadcast fully.

ABOUT THE AUTHOR

Troy Kirby has worked extensively as a professional broadcaster and writer for over 20 years. In his career, he's written feature stories for two daily newspapers, several weeklies, served as a sports communication professional at two athletic departments, has been a contributed for SEAT Magazine, founding managing editor of Ticketing Today and founder of the Tao of Sports website - which has provided business news to sports industry professionals from 2012 – 2018, with over 879 podcast episodes to date. Kirby has earned degrees from Seattle University, Eastern Washington University and Centralia College. He is originally from Lacey, Washington and has lived in various places throughout the West Coast. Mr. Kirby has worked in and around sports broadcasting for many years.

He has served as director of broadcasting for two collegiate athletic departments, training willing students on the finer points of sportscasting. He was named KCED Sportscaster of the Year in 2003, KCED Announcer of the Year and KCED Best New Announcer in 2001. Mr. Kirby has worked at three commercial radio stations as on-air talent, 1030 KMAS, 97.7 KFMY, 99.3 KAYO, conducted hundreds of livestream broadcasters of local high school and semi-pro sporting events, and executive produced / hosted a 49-episode season of a local public affairs channel, TVW, during the 2020 Washington State legislative session.

Made in the USA
Monee, IL
30 January 2022

89845308R00115